CHASE YOUR BRAVE

CHASE YOUR *brave*

ASPEN EMRY

Chase Your Brave
by Aspen Emry

Copyright © 2020 Aspen Emry

All rights reserved solely by the author. The author guarantees all contents are original and do not infringe upon the legal rights of any other person or work. No part of this book may be reproduced, stored in a retrieval system, or transmitted in any form or by any means—electronic, mechanical, photocopying, recording, or otherwise—without expressed written permission of the author.

While this book is a true account and based on facts, memories, and personal family documents and photos, the conversations recounted are not word-for-word. The stories have been recreated from memories to give the reader a better sense of the individuals involved.

ISBN (paperback): 978-0-578-76759-8

Library of Congress Control Number: 2020921603

Editor: Kara D. Starcher
Front cover design: Josh Aul, Nexlevel Design, LLC, www.nexleveldesign.com

Scripture quotations marked NIV are from the HOLY BIBLE, NEW INTERNATIONAL VERSION (NIV)®, copyright © 1973, 1978, 1984 by Biblica, Inc.™ Used by permission of Zondervan Publishing House. All rights reserved.

Scripture quotations marked ESV are from the ESV® Bible (The Holy Bible, English Standard Version®), copyright © 2001 by Crossway, a publishing ministry of Good News Publishers. Used by permission. All rights reserved.

29 28 27 26 25 24 23 22 21 20   1 2 3 4 5

*To my loving husband, Brent, and our five children
Logan, Mason, Parker, Owen, and Hazel.
And to our five babies that are in the arms of Jesus—
Samuel, Hope, Eli, Faith, and Bea.
I love you all to the moon and back
and will continue to be brave for you.*

contents

1 Chase Your Brave 1

2 Know Your Worth 9
   Brave Worthiness

3 Decide Your Why 19
   Brave Change

4 Say Yes 33
   Brave Fear

5 Let Go 45
   Brave Surrender

6 Listen To Your Gut 61
   Brave Intuition

7 Stay The Course 69
   Brave Commitment

8 Seek Support 83
   Brave Relationships

9 Think Outside The Box 93
   Brave Parenting

10 Tell Your Story 109
   Brave Faith

11 Choose All Of It.. 123
   Brave Purpose

Acknowledgments 135

About The Author 141

CHAPTER ONE

chase your brave

*"You keep him in perfect peace
whose mind is stayed on you,
because he trusts in you."*
Isaiah 26:3 (ESV)

A FEW YEARS AGO I was brain dumping on a large pink legal pad about all the things that encompass who I am and what I stand for. I was writing words that described me at my core and what impact I have on this world. I wrote words, such as *gratitude, ambitious, hopeful, trustworthy, integrity, mother, friend, empathetic*, and so many others. I wrote phrases down as well, like "mom on a mission" and "goal getter." I was working to put into words my life motto or mantra, and this exercise was helping me through that process.

On the pages of this notepad where I continued writing all the words and phrases that popped into my head, I scribbled the words *Chase Your Brave* in quick cursive letters...and then I dropped the pen. That was it. Three simple words. Chase. Your. Brave. Chase after those things in life that make you brave. The best and brightest things come from brave steps and big bold actions. Chase after the experiences that require bravery. Chase the opportunity that's through the brave doorway.

I am not someone who claims to have it all together or who claims she is the queen of big bold steps, but my life is an open book. I am excited to share what I have learned about bravery and how it's truly transformed my life and impacted the lives of so many others because of that transformation.

Before we start, I want you to know that I haven't always been that woman who stands in front of a crowd training others or who desired to write a book divulging intimate thoughts about her life. Years ago, I was that shy little girl you probably remember from elementary school. I was slightly embarrassed by my unusual name in a classroom full of Jennifers, Christinas, and Jamies, and even more embarrassed about my buck teeth. When I look back at my elementary school photos with my pursed lips covering my teeth and the shy "almost" smile, I just want to hug that sweet little girl and whisper some uplifting words into her little ears.

For most of my early life, I was timid and fearful. I grew up in the 80s where fear of the Cold War and so much uncertainty politically was enough to scare any little one who overheard too many adult conversations or too much news. In seventh grade, a light bulb somehow switched on inside of me. A girl in one of my classes exuded such confidence and spunk that we all couldn't help but take notice. I decided one day to step out of my shell and march up to her and say hi. We became fast friends and somehow just being near her gave me a boost of confidence in myself. Little by little, I opened up and my self-confidence started growing.

During my senior year of high school, I decided to let the university pair me up with a stranger rather than a friend the following year for my room assignment in the dorms. That decision led to a great friendship and boosted my self-confidence by essentially throwing me into the "social deep-end" of college life and forced me to make brand new friends from day one.

As I took some brave steps outside my comfort zone during my younger years, I grew from each step. Looking back now, each of these examples and many others seem kind of small and insignificant. However, sometimes in life, when looking back, we realize that the things we *thought* were small were actually the things *that mattered the most*. They weren't so small after all. What I was learning behind the scenes was that bravery paid off. It would have been easier to stay at my own desk in class and not risk the rejection of a new friend, but by stepping out of my little bubble, I gained confidence and a new friendship. It would have been much more comfortable to buddy up in the dorms with a lifelong friend, but by stepping out bravely, a whole new world opened up for me. I learned firsthand what it meant to be a "grown-up" and what it was like to work together with strangers in new situations.

Those early, seemingly small decisions set a precedent for much larger choices later on. I didn't recognize what was happening at the time, but I kept trusting the Lord with decisions. My past is full of examples where I was given a choice between taking the obvious route—the path of least resistance, the path that didn't have as much uncertainty—OR taking the path that had more unknowns, but a much greater chance of reward and growth. Day by day, month by month, and decision by decision, I continued stepping out in faith. I kept trusting that the Lord would help me over the next hill or mountain even when I couldn't see the other side.

By the time I was thirty, I realized that every wonderful blessing in my life came from my willingness to do something brave. On a personal, physical, mental, and spiritual level, everything good that happened to me occurred outside my comfort zone, outside the safe space of familiarity. Every single thing that has been good in my life came out of bravery rather than indecision and timidity. Recognizing these facts was revolutionary for me.

Everything changed when I started seeing the puzzle of my life and how each piece fit perfectly together. I looked at my husband and thought, "I wouldn't have you if it weren't for some brave decisions I made at twenty-one." I looked at each of my children and realized that each one of them existed because of my willingness to bravely trust the journey the Lord had us on. I examined my career, and my jaw dropped. Gratitude filled my heart when I saw the intricate pathway of brave choices I had made along the way to get to where I am now.

God saw the big picture the whole time while I faced only one decision at a time. All along the way, He gave me options to settle and opportunities to leap over. Those leaps were when the biggest blessings came. The leaps across the fire, through the unknowns, and during uncertain situations are when God showed me how big He really is and what living a brave, faith-filled life really looks like.

But let's take a step backward for a moment. What if you didn't do like I did and step out bravely as a child or even a young adult? What if you aren't currently living that brave, faith-filled life? Is it too late? Not at all. You have the choice to chase your brave, but what exactly does that mean?

- Bravery is not carelessness. It's confidence.
- Chasing your brave isn't making rash decisions. It's making choices based on faith.
- Living bravely isn't *not* considering others' thoughts and opinions. It's trusting in yourself enough to follow your calling even when others don't seem to understand. It's not your job to make them see. It's your job to walk the path that you're called to walk.
- Being brave doesn't mean there is no fear. Brave means feeling the fear and then choosing to take the leap anyway.
- Brave living doesn't mean you have a full map and strategy laid out and then make your decision. Bravery means knowing what could be, what might be, and having the strength to go for it, knowing that all things are possible.
- Chasing your brave isn't the easy way, but it is the way that

leads to living the life you were called to live.
- Chasing your brave means recognizing that you don't have all the answers to "how" something will work out, and trusting that, with faith and action on your part, the "how" will show up.

Chasing your brave allows room for God to work miracles in your life. When you make brave leaps where you don't have total control of the outcome, you leave space for God to prove his faithfulness. You also reinforce the truth that you are fully able to survive situations outside your comfort zone. You quickly learn that you don't simply survive, you thrive in the moments. Your confidence in yourself grows, your belief in your worth and calling expands, and you see regular confirmation of God's divine plan.

Chasing your brave is not easy. Brave decisions are often misunderstood by those around you. It's often uncomfortable and against the norm. If chasing your brave was always easy, everyone would do it, and we would not call it bravery. However, chasing your brave is like a muscle. It grows stronger and stronger with repeated use. Just like lifting weights or pushing your body to its limits demonstrates to you what your body is capable of, making brave decisions repeatedly reinforces to you what you are capable of. It reminds you that you do have what it takes to get through situations that aren't always easy.

When you exercise this muscle, choosing the brave path—the faith path—becomes your new norm. You become what others call fearless. You make an impact. You inspire others around you by showing them what's possible. You may not set out to inspire, but you do. You show people what's possible. You become the friend, the mother, the wife, the neighbor, the co-worker, and the sister that reminds the women around you of what they are capable of.

Are you ready to chase your brave?

✥

If you love authenticity and real raw emotion, then this book is for you. Get ready to see inside my heart and soul as I share several personal examples of times in my life where chasing my brave was the only option for me. You'll see just how much growth and faith it took to make brave decisions in many different areas of my life. My life reflects my life with God, but you don't have to believe in Him to chase your own brave (although He would make it all the sweeter for you!). No matter what your faith is, this book contains personal examples and action steps that will encourage you to chase your brave as you contemplate what's next for you. Whether you are looking for clarity on a career path, confirmation on relationship decisions, or something more, I want to help you dig deep for those answers within.

My hope is that through these pages you unpack some of your inner struggles. My prayer for you is that you recognize some areas where your worries have kept you locked up rather than flying free. My hope is that you see that I am a woman just like you who had some really big dreams that I just needed to, and continue to need to, chase my brave to achieve. My desire is that you would discover examples in your own life that demonstrate times you have chased your brave, perhaps unknowingly, and lived courageously and what that has meant for you. So, grab a cup of coffee and a cozy blanket as you join me on this journey of chasing our brave. You were created for such a time as this.

CHAPTER TWO

know your worth

*"I praise you because I am fearfully and wonderfully made;
your works are wonderful, I know that full well."*
Psalm 139:14 (NIV)

BRAVE WORTHINESS

What if I don't feel worthy of being brave?

What if my childhood was messed up?

What if my marriage or job is on the rocks?

What if I've been broken down in life?

> I can fail, and I am still worthy.
> I can take a breath, take time for myself,
> or make a mistake, and I am still valuable.

THE DOUGH ON MY HANDS felt sticky and warm. I couldn't wait to eat the delicious homemade bread in just a couple of hours. My sister Ashley, my stepsister Jillian, and I were happily chatting away as we worked the dough between our fingers on our antique kitchen table.

I glanced at Ashley and said, "Remember that time when we were at mom's house and we made those homemade—"

"You mean at *Deb's* house?" My stepmom snapped at me before I could finish my sentence with "chocolate peanut butter cups that were so good and so messy,"

Uh-oh. I had done it.

You see, Ashley and I were not allowed to call our biological mother "mom" in front of our stepmom. We had been told to call her "Deb." My stepmom had said hundreds of times, "Your mom is 'Deb the Web' because she's a spider who weaves her nasty web."

Yeah, I know, terrible words to say to a child. They broke my heart. I loved my mom, and those words hurt. Because I was young, I didn't fully grasp what my stepmom meant by her words or why she insisted on calling our mom "Deb the Web." Now, as an adult, I understand that my stepmom was allowing her own adult feelings toward my dad's ex-wife, my mom, to spill over into how she talked to my sister and me. I knew nothing about the details of my parents' divorce at the time, nor did I want to. I just knew I loved my mom, and she loved me.

My biological parents' marriage had been brief and rocky, ending before I was six. Both remarried quickly, and we ended up at my dad's house with our stepmom a lot of the time. He had met my stepmom at church, and both had two little kids. Truth be told, they needed each other. He needed help with his children, and she needed a provider and help with hers. For us kids, our new second family was awesome in so many ways. I got an instant big brother and a new sister that was only one year younger than me. We liked to tell new friends that we were twins! Being poor was so much easier with the four of us kids. We had built-in playmates to do life with and to create the craziest inside jokes with. These are jokes that we *still* laugh about today! Our childhoods had lots of these good times, but some things happened, like "Deb the Web," that left deep scars that would shape me into the woman I became years down the road.

One day when I was fifteen, my stepsister, Jillian, and I were having a discussion with my stepmom about something. Honestly, I don't remember the topic. Boys? School? Politics? It could have been anything. I know it seems unusual to write about a conversation that I don't quite remember, but it wasn't the topic of conversation that stuck with me. What was said to me during that conversation took my breath away and has impacted every one of my relationships, both professional and personal, since that moment.

As I finished expressing my thought on whatever the topic was, and Jillian nodded with me in agreement, my stepmom looked right at me and pointed as she said, "*You* are not old enough to have an opinion of your own, and when you are, I'll let you know." She wasn't yelling or angry. She just stated it as fact, letting me know that my opinion, on any matter really, was irrelevant due to my age.

As a fifteen-year-old, type A, firstborn, people pleaser, I stood there stunned. Needless to say, our conversation was immediately over. In that moment, I learned *never* to share anything that I thought or felt on a subject ever again.

Yes, this was just one moment in time, but in all honesty, it was the theme in my relationship with my stepmom. This was a *truth* that carried throughout this relationship in our interactions. Sure, we had great times and good memories. We had so much fun picking strawberries out of the strawberry patch my stepmom had creatively planted in an old concrete horse trough. We enjoyed s'mores around our campfire while we sat on old tree stumps, sang songs to my dad's acoustic guitar, and watched fireflies light up all around us. She taught us to bake the world's best pumpkin bars and roll out the perfect sugar cookies. My memories could fill endless pages, but those good memories never took away the underlying pain. The pain of feeling unworthy. The pain of feeling like I didn't matter and my thoughts didn't matter.

As I went through junior high and high school, I had lots of friends and excelled in school. I felt compelled to perform and always give 100 percent. The thought of getting less than an A made my stomach turn, and the anxiety that surrounded friendships and being "liked" was insomnia-inducing. I so wanted to connect with others, but again, I didn't feel worthy because my opinion and thoughts did not matter. I was embarrassed to speak up or challenge anyone else's way of thinking.

It's only now as an adult that I can look back and see how much of my life was spent trying to please others and to feel like *I mattered*. About ten years ago, I finally pinpointed so much from my past as a reason for my present. I can't tell you how many times I have said to my husband, "I don't need you to fix this. I just need you to hear me." Dozens of times I have entered an interaction with a colleague thinking "I don't expect to always get my way, and I *know* that I am not always right, but I just want to know that my ideas have been

Know this, my friend,
you are worthy
to chase your brave.

You. Are. Worthy.

heard." I have felt such elation after leaving a conversation where the outcome was not what I had hoped for when I went into it, but my thoughts and ideas were given thoughtful consideration and possibly revamped or saved for a later date.

My friends know that I am naturally self-reflective. As a self-proclaimed personal development junkie, I'll be the first to tell you all the areas I want to grow in. Self-reflection has shown me that I suffer from feelings of unworthiness stemming from the earliest times in childhood where I was told, quite literally, that my thoughts and feelings didn't matter. That who I am was not enough. That I am not enough. It may surprise you, or maybe not after what I have shared, that I was even told as a child that my name was stupid. I was assured that someday I would grow up and be allowed to legally change my name to my middle name of Nicole. This brought such confusion and hurt. I mean, I knew that some kids at school had fun teasing me as they chanted "Aspirin!" on the school playground. But I had dozens more people tell me that "Aspen" was a beautiful, unique name. Once again, my self-esteem tanked, and I felt like not only was I physically this buck-toothed, awkward, young girl who wasn't capable of thinking for herself, but to top it all off, I had the stupidest name ever given to a child.

So, what changed for me? What happened to me? I recognized the lies I grew up believing and replaced them with *truth*. God's truth. The truth that I had come to know and believe. My Bible tells me that I am created in God's image and am fearfully and wonderfully made. Scripture assures me that I am a treasure more valuable than jewels.

I started speaking truth to myself. (Yes, I talk to myself, and you know you do, too!) Think about it. What have you told yourself today? Have you told yourself that you really need to start losing weight? Have you scolded yourself for something you didn't get done or called yourself a failure? We have an inner dialogue going on in our minds all the time. Sometimes it's very active, and we're keenly aware of it. We may even blurt something out loud like "Darn it, Julie, you're late again! Why can't you get your act together and get somewhere on time for once?" But, other times, it's an inner dialogue humming quietly in the background. For years, I had that quiet internal dialogue. It was just this underlying thing I couldn't quite pinpoint until I started asking myself "Why? Why does it bother me so much when this happens? Why do I feel this way? Why do I hesitate to say what I *really* think about this situation?"

Once I understood what I was doing, and how I was diminishing myself, I then had the power to stop it by speaking truth. You know what the truth is? My opinions and feelings *do* matter. My ideas are valuable. What I want out of life and relationships is significant and important. I am worthy of love and respect. I am worthy of time and attention. I am capable of success in any area that I decide to pursue. These are true for you, too.

The other step I took was choosing to forgive my stepmom, Marlee, and love her in spite of any hurt she had caused. I chose to give her grace and learn from and grow through the things I went through. I know that hurt people often hurt people, and I didn't want to cause more hurt. I set boundaries in our relationship as I grew older into adulthood. When she let me know that her recent medical news wasn't good, I spent the last three weeks of her life with her, helping so many loved ones care for her and choosing to be a bright spot for her in her last days. I forgave her long before that time in our lives, and I'm grateful I did because holding on to the pain and bitterness of unforgiveness would have only made me more miserable. I know my God forgives me, so I choose to forgive others. With that forgiveness comes such freedom. Was my relationship with Marlee perfect after I forgave her? No, but we had boundaries, and we loved each other in our own way.

Yes, I spent years of my life feeling unworthy, like I wasn't good enough and I didn't matter, but the Bible says in Jeremiah 29:11, "For I know the plans I have for you, declares the Lord, plans for welfare and not for evil, to give you a future and a hope." In God's eyes, I was worth planning for! He planned a future for me. I was and am worthy. I was not a victim of my upbringing or my circumstance.

And you know what? You are not a victim. You are worthy. God has planned a future for you too. What truths do you need to speak over your life to believe in yourself? Do you need to offer forgiveness to someone for wrongs they did? Don't allow negativity and unworthiness to beat you down in life and destroy your dreams. Don't allow the opinions of others make you question who you are. Get in touch with your core values—who are *you*? Who do you want to be *for you*? Trust your inner self and build a foundation strong enough so that no one can make you question your value. You are worthy.

I have learned these truths: My self-worth and value are not tied to my accomplishments or my performance. They are not tied to my appearance or my contribution to anything specific. My value on this earth isn't tied to my possessions, the number of likes on social media, or crossing off a lengthy to-do list. My value comes from above and from within. This gives me so much peace—peace that

I am free to just be me in spite of what anyone else thinks or does. I can fail, and I am still worthy. I can take a breath, take time for myself, or make a mistake, and I am still valuable. No one gets to tell me that I am a mistake or call me stupid. I don't need to prove myself to anyone, and neither do you.

CHAPTER THREE

decide your why

*"See, I am doing a new thing!
Now it springs up; do you not perceive it?
I am making a way in the wilderness
and streams in the wasteland."*
Isaiah 43:19 (NIV)

BRAVE CHANGE

If you believe you are worthy of chasing *your* brave,
what is standing in your way?

What obstacle or challenge do you need to overcome?

> Be brave in pursuit of you.
> Bravely chase after those mini-milestones
> and watch the big picture of your best self unfold.

It's HARD TO THINK BACK to a time in my life when I *wasn't* consumed with thoughts of body image issues and losing weight. I remember being really young, back when they used to weigh you in gym class, and being mortified to see seventy-seven pounds on the scale when my closest friends were still in the sixty-five-pound range. I didn't understand that everyone grows differently and that my extra couple of inches in height meant that I was just a bit ahead of the curve. On the outside, I looked just like everyone else, but on the inside, I was already beating myself up and wishing I was more "ideal." I became so ridiculously self-conscious about all things relating to my body, and I was critical of what I thought were my flaws.

By the summer after seventh grade, I started dabbling in dieting. As a thirteen-year-old, I knew nothing about calories, grams of fat, or carbohydrates. I just assumed that to lose weight you must eat less, so I enlisted my twelve-year-old sister to join the new diet program I was developing. I decided a "diet" lunch for us would be five chips, instead of two handfuls, and half of a sandwich, instead of a whole. My sister made it a day and realized that riding horses and playing in our tree house was more fun than rationing food and counting the minutes until bedtime and the day of dieting was over. Somehow, I managed to stick with this awkward diet plan (randomly deciding what constituted a diet portion) for the entire summer. When I strolled into school ten pounds lighter on a hot August morning, I heard one of my guy friends exclaim, "Wow, you've lost weight!" Truth be told, I didn't really even need to lose the weight, but I felt special, worthwhile, and like my new skinnier self was somehow "better" than the old me that had walked out of the building at the end of the previous school year.

Do you have memories like that? Maybe a moment where you can pinpoint the beginning of some of your struggles? Maybe that time when you started compromising or losing track of your core values? Do you remember where the teeter-totter started for you? Do you sense that it is time for a change in your life?

I'm going to talk about Brave Change in the context of my weight loss journey simply because that journey has had a profound effect on me. However, if weight loss isn't your thing, don't be discouraged. Take the steps in this chapter and apply them to whatever obstacle you need to overcome in order to have the self-confidence you need to chase your brave. My body image struggle started at a young age, and more than likely, whatever obstacle you need to overcome has been deeply rooted in your life for years and years. My prayer is that my journey will help you see that you *can* stand up and take the steps to change even the most ingrained habits.

I think it's safe to say that every woman, at some point in her life, will struggle with her weight or her body image. Society bombards us with images of skinny models, moms whose bodies bounce back perfectly after childbirth, and all sorts of ideal bodies every single day. And let's face it, those ads and messages can become overwhelming, especially when we are struggling. They can eat away at our self-worth and help us forget that we are fearfully and wonderfully made by God like we talked about in Chapter One.

From the ages of thirteen to twenty-three, I swung on the pendulum of gaining and losing ten to twenty pounds at any given time. On the outside, no one would have suspected that I had any food issues because I wasn't walking around overweight. I would diet and often over exercise to get thin for spring break, a wedding, or some event in my life. I wasn't creating new lifestyle habits; I was simply changing things for a season. My twenties brought babies and, of course, some weight gain during pregnancy, but I got serious after each baby and lost the excess forty to fifty pounds that I was carrying each time.

In my late thirties after my fifth baby, I accepted an exciting job that allowed me to travel all the time, meet new people, see new places, *and* take my baby girl with me. What I didn't plan on was the job adding an extra fifty pounds to the already fifty extra pounds of baby weight I was carrying around.

For about four years I watched the scale go up and up and up. I realized I was eating my feelings. I ate when I was sad, happy, excited, stressed. I ate to enjoy the food and the new friends in each city I traveled to. During that time, I owned a company and continued traveling and eating for any reason I could think of. Tired at the airport? Grab some chocolate! Bummed to go back to the hotel room and missing my five kiddos back home? Eat some chips and a candy bar while watching reruns of *Friends* to numb the feeling of being sad. Have you ever done these things or is it just me?

I know food is enjoyable and often a centerpiece of celebrations, and there's nothing wrong with that, but I was treating food as my best friend. My companion. My choice above all others. Have you ever splurged on some dessert or indulged when you were already full and said to yourself "I am going to regret this later!" because you knew that you didn't really need it? Yeah, that was me for *four* years. I had experienced parts of that feeling since seventh grade, but it was heightened during those four years when I put on the extra one-hundred pounds.

Sadly, food had me in a prison of sorts. Deep inside, I was *struggling*. I felt so gross and unlovable. No one on the outside knew my pain, but surely they saw the excess weight to some degree. I still dressed the part of a successful business owner, spoke on stages, and spent lots of time socializing professionally. My kids still had a mom that showed up to games and had silly dance parties in the kitchen. But I wasn't living my best life, my fullest life. I didn't feel like an active participant in all the things going on around me. I felt like a failure. I failed each and every week that I said, "Monday I will start" or "This time is going to be different." Sure, I would lose ten to twenty pounds here or there over a few weeks, but then a trip would come or a birthday or any excuse that I could think of to break whatever I was doing to lose weight. I would crumble. This perpetuated more overeating, closet eating, secret eating, and shame eating.

Then, I hit rock bottom. I finally got sick and tired of huffing and puffing, not sleeping great, buying size 24 clothes, and so many other things. That's when I decided I needed to change. I didn't know precisely what "change" meant, but I knew I needed something different than where I was. Rock bottom is a hard place to be, and thankfully, there's only one direction left when you're there—up.

What does rock bottom look like? It's those moments where you feel shame, hopelessness, and unworthiness, and it's possibly that place you keep hidden from everyone else. Take a moment and think about specific moments that are part of your rock bottom. Now, go grab a pen and paper and write down that thing you want to change in your life more than anything else.

One day my four teenage sons and I were looking at old photos together. We were scrolling through my phone looking for a few pictures from about five years prior when Logan exclaimed, "Wow, Mom! I don't even recognize you there!"

I literally fought back tears as the realization hit me that my kids only knew me as this overweight, out-of-shape, "eat my feelings" mom. They didn't even recognize me in the photo when I was thin and fit. This realization hit me in the core because a huge part of my goal as a mother, long before I even had children, was to be a fit, healthy, energetic mom. This wasn't because of any ideal that society had placed before me. It was simply because being a mother was such a huge deal to me. The biggest deal of my life. I didn't want to just let those brief years of kids being in my home pass me by.

And here, that was exactly what was happening. Sure, I was as present as possible with my kids, but, for example, I wasn't out at the beach with them as much as I could have been. Putting on a bathing suit, stuffing myself into a beach chair, and trying to get up from the chair discouraged me from being present and having fun with my kids in the spontaneous way that I wanted to, while being comfortable in my own skin.

The other nail in the proverbial coffin of my "rock bottom" was hammered in more than once on an airplane. I spent a lot of time flying because of the nature of my work. I can hardly put into words what it felt like to be sitting next to a sweet chatty person (I love talking to my seat companions!) and have them ask me "What do *you* do for a living?" You see, inside I am so very proud to be a founder and CEO of a global health and wellness company with fabulous supplements and products. But to say that, at one-hundred-plus pounds overweight, to the person next to me was nothing short of utter humiliation. I felt like such a hypocrite. I felt so ashamed not representing my brand the way I wanted to. That, my friend, was so hard and was part of my turning point.

Enough was enough. I was no longer willing to be the business owner who wasn't representing her core values about health. I would no longer stand for being the mom who couldn't race my kids up and down the beach or walk for hours through amusement parks at the same pace. I wanted to feel amazing when we were out and about enjoying fishing, boating, sports, and all of life's adventures. I decided that what I wanted long term was more than what I wanted in the short term. What I mean by that is I wanted health, vitality, congruency in my beliefs and actions about health, and active days with my kids *more* than M&Ms, powdered donuts, and Cadbury eggs from morning until night. I also realized how little gratification, if any, I was getting from stuffing my face and beating myself up day after day.

Those things I wanted? They were only part of my reason "why" I had to change and "why" I had to lose weight. If you've ever tried to lose weight, you probably knew an approximate (or in some cases, exact) number of pounds you wanted to lose. Typically, we focus on that number. We want to lose twenty pounds. We want to lose thirty pounds. Or we might have a dress in mind that we want to wear or an event coming up in two months that we want to feel better for. But usually, that's about as deep as it goes. Most people don't dig deep enough to find those underlying reasons "why" making a change is so important, so necessary.

So, I want you to dig deep here with me. Why do you want to make your big change? Think about those moments again where you felt shame, hopelessness, or unworthiness. What is your motivation for change? For me, I would have said, "I want to lose one-hundred pounds so I can be more active and present with my kids and we can make more exciting memories. I want to feel comfortable and energized in our daily activities."

But let's not stop there. Let's ask ourselves why *again*. Why do you want those things? My "why" question looked something like "Why do I want to feel comfortable and energized during my daily adventures with my kids?" My answer to that was "because for as long as I can remember I wanted to be a mother. My kids are only in my home for such a brief time. This time will pass quickly. I don't want to live with the regret of choosing my snacks and my comfort food over our times together."

Do you see how this gets deep quickly? I did this same exercise with other painful areas, my other "why's." I dug into the emotions of how it felt to not be an example of health and wellness as a company owner. I felt such a responsibility to all the Brand Partners sharing our products every day that I felt convicted to change. I needed to be the best that I could be for them because they deserved that from me.

As you connect with these deeper reasons, you'll want to take some time to truly picture in your mind what it will be like when, not *if*, you reach your goal. What will it feel like to reach your ideal body? Not some ideal you've seen on TV, but that healthy place that is perfect for you. How will it feel to slip on that comfortable pair of jeans that have been too tight for a few years? How will it feel to walk down the street with no pain in your knees? How will you feel about yourself when you've accomplished this personal goal?

As I dug deep for all the reasons "why" I was going to, once and for all, stop saying "I will start Monday" or "This new plan will finally work for me," I felt my commitment rising. I started thinking about what it would feel like to sit in that airplane seat and proudly share about my career when asked. I pictured what it would feel like to spend an exhilarating day at an amusement park keeping up with the kids! I envisioned what it would feel like to shop for clothes at any store I wished. I thought about how proud I would be of myself for achieving this goal and how good it would feel to know that I had prioritized my health. I knew that there would be some healing along the way, and I was in for the long haul. I was ready to be *me* again.

I want to stress that part of this whole weight loss process for me was sorting through society's beliefs, and my core feelings, emotions, and desires, as well as getting super honest about what the future would look like if I stayed stuck versus got it together. I mention society because as much as it bothered me to be seen in a swimming suit or to answer questions about my career in health and wellness, my reasons for those things bothering me so much were *internal*. I knew, at the end of the day, if someone judged me for my weight as a wellness company owner, that was on them. I knew that I was still an awesome mom to my kids in spite of my weight and that *they* weren't sitting around judging me for it. I might have been winded at the amusement parks, but we were still out living life. The inadequate feelings were inside of *me*. This was about *me* wanting more. *I* expected more of myself in my career. I had committed to more in motherhood. I wanted to be healthier at my age. My commitment to losing weight was very much an internal process of making my goals and dreams a reality. I wanted to be an example to others of what is possible when you decide to overcome an obstacle and reach a goal.

I'm sure some of you might be wondering how I started the weight loss process, but I am not going to spend time in this book explaining my process and dishing recipes and workouts. Why not? Because I want you to make brave changes in the areas of your life that matter the most to you and not get sidetracked by a weight loss program. Plus, I want to give you action steps to take *right now* for how to make a long-term change. It's time for your breakthrough.

First, and we've already talked about this one, decide on your "why." This is the most important step, and it's got to be deeper than you've ever gone before. Grab that pen and paper from earlier and list at least five reasons why you want to change and are committed to your goal.

Second, break your end goal into small goals. I believe everyone should do this, no matter how huge your goal is. It's easier to give yourself a mental pep talk when you are close to reaching a small goal of losing twenty-five pounds than saying "Well, I've been at this for four months and still haven't lost one-hundred pounds." When I started on my journey toward losing one-hundred pounds, I didn't focus on that big number. I viewed it as losing ten pounds, ten times. I just kept thinking, "I am losing ten pounds. I can lose ten pounds." Focusing on the small goals was truly a game-changer for me because focusing on the big goal for too long caused so much defeat. Previously, I couldn't even enjoy a twenty-pound loss because I felt like such a failure for having eighty more pounds to go. But I could do small goals—ten pounds, ten times!

How do we change other areas of our lives that might not have a measurable goal like ten pounds? Maybe you're a Negative Nancy who views the glass as half-empty all the time and you want to change to a positive attitude. Rather than saying "I will never speak another negative word again for the rest of my life," make the change day by day. Commit to speaking one positive thought out loud every day for the first week. Then add in two positive thoughts. Or maybe your goal involves a huge career change. Sit down and list out the steps you need to accomplish in order to successfully change careers. Make those steps or a combination of steps your small goals.

The third action step is to tell at least one person about your commitment to bettering yourself. This person should be someone that will hold you accountable, and someone who is safe and that you trust to not kick you if you fall. I told my kids, my husband, and my two best friends to start, and then soon after went public in front of thousands on social media. That's what worked for me, but you've got to do what's best for you and what you are comfortable with. Start by telling one person.

Fourth, celebrate the small wins. Remember those small goals from the second step? Those are reason for celebration! Please, do not wait until you've reached your ultimate goal before you pat yourself on the back. Each small step in the right direction matters. Look at yourself in the mirror and tell yourself how very proud you are as you journey toward whom you've always wanted to be and whom you have always been deep inside that you are now uncovering. When I was posting updates to my social media about my weight loss, I'd say, "I am down 75.4 pounds today, not just 75 because I worked hard for that .4!" I celebrated that .4 because it was important to me, and for every ten-pound mini-milestone, I gave myself a special reward. One reward was a facial, another one was a massage, and another was a pair of earrings I had wanted for a while. You might treat yourself to a new audiobook, a pedicure, or a new movie that you've been wanting to see. However big or small your rewards are is up to you; just be sure to celebrate.

Finally, don't give up. New actions take time to become actual habits. Be willing to fail and start again, fail and start again, and do it all over as many times as you need to. During the process of losing weight, I've stumbled, fallen, and gotten back up to start again. To me, I'm on a journey, not just a one-stop destination. Stay committed to your goal and keep on trying. When you stumble, as we all do, please go back to your why's, those reasons you said "yes" to yourself this time. Many times when you revisit your why *before* you stumble, it keeps you in check. I've often asked myself "What do I want more right now—to eat that pizza everyone else is eating (when I am not even hungry) or to hit my next mini-milestone?" or "What do I want more—a second helping of something I just ate or to feel energetic and strong as I play at the beach with the kids?" Oftentimes, just those simple questions and taking the time to pause were enough to keep me right on track. Remember your why.

I've also learned that it's okay to stumble. You're going to hit roadblocks, and you're likely going to visit some emotional valleys as you make lifestyle changes. Move forward one day at a time. This journey isn't about perfection; it's about progress. This is your path, your journey, to a better version of you.

My hope for you, dear friend, is that you get to the heart of the matter and decide that today is your day. Not Monday, but today. It's time for a fresh start. It's time to uncover the "you" that is right there. Be brave in pursuit of *you*. Bravely chase after those mini-milestones and watch the big picture of your best self unfold. And remember that even if you stumble and fall short of your goal, you are still worthy. Do not allow failure to shape who you are. Stand back up and start over. You've got this!

CHAPTER FOUR

say yes

"Cast all your anxiety on him because he cares for you."
1 Peter 5:7 (NIV)

BRAVE FEAR

What if fears hold me back from my goal?

What is something you are so scared of that you would rather not try than to try and fail?

What if everything you've ever wanted, needed, and been called to do is on the other side of a powerfully brave decision?

> Bravery can become a habit that leads to all sorts of amazing opportunities.

I COULD FEEL THE SWEAT dripping down my palms as I gripped the armrest of my window seat on the already packed airplane. We hadn't even taken off yet, and I was already fighting panic. Truth be told, I was going off of a combined four hours of sleep over the previous three nights. I was an exhausted wreck. I glanced around the plane perplexed as I saw people already sleeping and others comfortably adjusting the reading light so the beam perfectly hit their book. "How are they not all terrified of dying right now? How can they possibly all be acting so *normal*? Do they not know that they are about to close the door?"

Years ago, on the way home from our Las Vegas wedding, my new husband and I experienced a flight with so much turbulence and, for me, so much anxiety that I exclaimed "I am never flying again!" The tragedy of 9/11 occurred nine months after that and solidified my commitment to not fly ever again. My debilitating fear turned into a life-altering phobia.

Those scenes and many others like them played out over and over for years every time I flew. I would have days of stress, worry, and catastrophic thinking leading up to the flight, moments of panic, and then breathe a sigh of relief when we touched down, actually shocked that we had made it. Something would happen to me on flights, and I couldn't help but think of the worst-case scenario and all the things that could go wrong. My imagination went absolutely crazy. Every bump, every bit of turbulence, every sound that I didn't understand only fed my fear and accentuated this belief that we were in danger. It wasn't even necessarily the height of the flight but more the feeling of being trapped that bothered me. I liken it to the experience of having a C-section. I'm a five-time C-section mom, and I remember laying there on that table each time thinking "Whatever happens, I am here for it! There is no turning back now!" During the C-section, there was nothing I could do about the situation I was in. Of course, I was excited to get a baby at the end of it, but the actual surgery experience terrified me. While on the plane, I feel the exact same way. I believe it honestly stems from control. It's the reason why one of the scariest parts of flying for me is when they shut the door. There is some sort of finality with that door locking in place. In that moment, I know that whatever happens, I need to get through it. Whether I'm scared, calm, or completely petrified, I need to get to the end of the flight somehow, some way.

After seven years of never taking a flight, I realized something had to be done. Not only had I missed my sister's wedding, driven twenty-four hours through the mountains seven months pregnant to attend a meeting for eight hours, and missed numerous opportunities for family vacations that were further away than a day's drive, but I was tired of letting my fear have complete control. I enlisted in an online class with books on flying, a consultation with a pilot who was also a licensed therapist, and some exercises to supposedly help the process of flying. I completed all the course materials perfectly, read additional supplemental books about how airplanes are constructed, and had a phone conversation with the pilot/therapist.

I reached the point where I was ready for that first post-course flight. I offered to pay for a flight for my good friend if she would accompany me on my first flight after seven years on the ground. My four-month-old baby would be joining us on the three-hour flight from Nebraska to Arizona. The online course warned that the exercises and coping mechanisms that I had learned wouldn't do much for the anticipatory anxiety, and the pilot/therapist explained during our phone consultation that I would likely still feel all the anxiety beforehand. This meant that I would have no idea if the course actually helped until I was on the airplane up in the air.

On a snowy February morning, we left at 3:30 in the morning to head for the airport. My stomach was literally in knots, and nausea kicked in on the way to the airport. I practiced positive self-talk the whole way there and just chose to believe that somehow everything was going to work, I would get on the airplane and make it to my destination, and it would somehow be better than it had been before.

I was in tears as we walked up to the ticket counter, and I cried my way through the whole airport. I have a feeling that people assumed I had just experienced a teary goodbye with the love of my life! I am sure they had no clue that they were tears of fear, stress, and worry over what was coming. I was lucky to have my little baby with me to snuggle up close as we started to walk on the plane. The moment I entered the plane the realization of what was happening started to take over. I stumbled briefly, and I'm slightly embarrassed to even share this part, I bumped into a flight attendant who was holding some things on a tray. I nearly dropped my baby, but thankfully another flight attendant was there to help steady us both. My friend kindly asked someone to hop up from the window seat so that I might have a chance to look out the window, and we prepared for take-off. While we were up in the air, I will say that many of the strategies I learned in the online course did help. I at least had made a big step in the whole process of conquering my fear, but my journey was far from over.

Over the next eight years, our family would take one or two trips a year by airplane. Honestly, I was not cured, but I was not letting my phobia keep us from taking a vacation. I still had a lot of anxiety in the days leading up to the flight and found myself holding back on some of the traveling we wanted to do. But, at least, I was taking a brave step in the right direction. I didn't let fear hold me back at this point, but it was still quite traumatic for me to fly anywhere. Sometimes, I still had a panic attack on the flight. I found ways to hide it from my children because I did not want to scare them. On one particular flight, the flight attendants actually moved my children to the back of the plane with my husband so they would not see me panicking. I wanted to protect them and not instill my fear of flying in them.

The next big leap that was completely life-changing, and ridiculously brave at the same time, came in the winter of 2017. My dream job was to work for a company to coach, train, lead, and mentor women all around the world who were working home-based businesses. For about seven years I had described this perfect job to those around me and prayed for an opportunity. I prayed that this dream job would have flexibility, the ability to work from home, great pay, and the ability to serve, share, and connect with women on a large scale.

In the winter of 2017, I landed an interview with a multi-million-dollar global company that had a position exactly like the one I had been praying for. But here's the catch, even though I would not need to relocate, the role would require an immense amount of travel. I was grateful that taking this position would allow me to take my one-year-old daughter along with me anywhere and everywhere, but I knew it would take an insurmountable amount of courage for me to take this job knowing that airplanes would no longer simply be a once or twice a year experience. I would be flying on ten to fifteen trips every month! I was excited about the idea of seeing different cities and meeting new people, taking my kids with me on some of these trips, and getting to serve, lead, and work in a role that was truly a dream come true. Even if I had to fly.

Choosing to accept the job or not was a pivotal moment in my life. I had some conversations with myself and gave myself some pep talks in my bathroom mirror. This was one of those life-defining moments, and I knew I had to choose wisely. Was I going to let this fear of flying, or, more accurately, a phobia of flying, hold me back from so much that I had dreamed of? Was I going to let this phobia keep me from a career that could be life-changing for our family and so many others? It was then that I realized just how important bravery was. The comfortable thing would have been to say to myself, "You don't need this job. Brent makes good money, you are home with the kids, and things are comfortable. Why put yourself under stress when you know you don't love to fly?" I knew that, even though I had strategies for coping, asking myself to fly consistently would stretch me beyond any limit. I would not have friends with me on flights. I would not have my husband there to hold my hand and be the voice of reason for me during turbulence. I would truly be on my own if I said "yes" to this job.

At this point, saying "yes" scared me, but in all honesty, saying "no" terrified me. I knew that saying "no" meant that I was letting fear control me. I was not trusting the Lord. I was not walking toward and through the doors that He was opening for me. I would be saying "no" to the prayers that God had specifically answered for me. So, the decision was a no-brainer. I needed to listen to this calling. I needed to say "yes" to the job. I needed to say "yes" for my family. And I needed to accept the job to prove to myself that I could do brave things. I could do hard things. I could do all things through Christ who strengthens me. I did not want to live a moment longer in the prison of this fear. I chose to chase my brave. I accepted the job, made my travel schedule for the very first month, and said to my husband, "It's go time! I will never conquer this if I don't try."

Those first months—I'm not going to sugarcoat this—were absolutely brutal. It was terrifying to fly with my daughter while battling the fear and anxiety inside. It was rough trying to care for her when I felt like I was crumbling. Each flight left me exhausted from the emotions of the experience, and yet I needed to walk into a meeting as the picture of confidence and enthusiasm.

Something that I did to help from the very first flight was to memorize the sounds, sights, and feelings I felt on the plane. I paid specific attention to everything and literally said to myself "This is normal." This was particularly helpful when a new sound, a new sight, or even a new turn or way of flying happened on a particular flight. In certain cities, I noticed that the plane ascended much more gradually than others. Arriving and departing from certain airports, I noticed that we often went quite a way out over the water before circling back. To a fearful flyer, any change from normal often brings fear, irrational thoughts, and panic. So, by paying particular attention to those things that seemed abnormal, I quickly realized that lots of those seemingly unusual happenings were just part of flying. By memorizing each new thing, it began to register as normal in my mind and to my body when I felt it again. This habit created more and more confidence in the process. This is going to sound very dramatic, but each time something scary happened and *I lived through it*, I added the event to the column in my brain titled "Normal things that happen on airplanes even though I don't understand why or particularly like them!" My fear dissipated some, and I wasn't caught off guard when something new happened on a flight.

I mentioned before that I utilized a lot of self-talk during flight. I was not someone who could sit and read books and fill myself with distractions. I was very present in the experience. Sitting by the window helped ground me somehow. I needed to see the land below and exactly where we were. I found myself saying over and over "We are on a highway in the sky. There are thousands of other planes up here right now bouncing around just like us. The pilots are following a perfectly planned path, and we will get there just fine!" This inner dialogue played over and over in my mind. I would remind myself of how normal the experience was. I thought of all the others just like me up in the air all around the world getting from one place to another. I reassured myself by thinking about the pilots and their families. This was a routine trip for them, and they longed to be home with their families later that same evening. I did whatever I could to normalize the experience and work through the fear.

When I have told parts of this story to others, they have asked why I simply did not drink some alcohol or take some medication on a flight. Those things seemed much easier to do rather than all the internal dialogue, strength, and personal effort that I needed to utilize on every flight. Please know that I am not knocking anyone who has used alcohol or anti-anxiety medication to get through a flight or a moment of stress, but for me, I knew I needed to face my fear head-on. I wanted to work through this thing that had held me back so much. And, honestly, I was afraid to mask my feelings with a glass of wine or something to take the edge off. You see, something about the process was very therapeutic for me. Yes, it took several months to even get to a place where panic wasn't even in the background. However, powering through it all and facing these fears head-on had an enormous impact on me.

On one particular flight, I had an epiphany. We were cruising at 37,000 feet, and I was looking out the window feeling quite scared and uneasy. I wasn't in a panic. This flight was probably the thirtieth of my new job, so I knew the ropes, but I was definitely feeling anxiety. Truth be told, I was beating myself up. I was looking around the plane looking at other people relaxing and even laughing with their seat companion having a good time. I thought to myself, "Why not me? What's wrong with me that I can't handle this the way that everyone else can?" At that moment I looked out the window and realized I was doing this. I was scared, but I was doing it. I was feeling the fear and doing it anyway. I was being brave. I didn't have to like it, and it was okay to be scared, but I wasn't letting the fear hold me back. I was chasing my brave in that moment, and that was my superpower. I thought about all the people who had laughed a nervous laugh when I told them about my accepting a new job and its travel requirements. I thought of other times in my life where I had said no to opportunities due to not feeling adequate or some sort of fear that kept me from being all in. I accepted the fact—no, embraced the fact—that being brave and doing something huge did not mean the complete absence of fear. It was okay to boldly go toward my dreams in spite of fear, not only in the absence of fear. My friend, that right there was mind-blowing to me. The depth of what that statement meant pierced me to the soul. I didn't have to get to a place where I loved flying, wanted to take flying lessons, and tried jumping out of airplanes. I was doing something very important even though I was doing it scared. But I was doing it.

As women, I know many of us struggle with some form of perfectionism. We tend to think that if we can't do it perfectly or exactly how we think it should be done, then it's easier not to even try. In that moment on the airplane, I realized that it wasn't about being the perfect airline passenger but it was being perfectly me in that moment and doing it in spite of any fear.

We all have fears. We've all had times in our lives where it has been much easier just to stay in what I call the "safe bubble," otherwise known as our "comfort zone." But what have we missed because we stayed in that bubble? Think about something that you know you want to do, need to do, or are called to do that scares you. Is there a skill you'd like to learn? A job that you'd like to take? Or an adventure that you'd like to go on? It's okay to go after something even if you're a bit scared or even if you don't have all the answers. You don't have to have it all figured out. Take one bold step at a time and push fear to the side.

Here are some key questions that can help you find bravery in the face of some of your deepest fears.

- What is it that you want or are called to do that you haven't said "yes" to? What's your big change from Chapter Two? Identifying and being honest about this piece is so important.
- What do *you* need to chase your brave? Remember this is about you and not the needs of everyone else.
- Why is this thing so important? Why are you afraid? What is it exactly that you are afraid of?

- What is the worst that's going to happen? What are some of the amazing things that could happen when you say yes to yourself, step out in bravery, and do that thing that you've always wanted to do? When I am on an airplane and I feel that fear creeping in, I simply remind myself of who and what is waiting on the other end. When I was on that C-section table, and there was no way out until it was over, I reminded myself over and over of the bundle of joy that would be placed in my arms at the end. We must not let ourselves get so wrapped up in the what if's that we forget to see the triumphs that happen on the other side.
- How will you feel inside when you work through this fear and take this brave step?

I will tell you from experience that one brave decision leads to other brave decisions. Chasing your brave is like a muscle. The more you use it, the easier it is to step outside that safe bubble, that comfort zone. Bravery can become a habit that leads to all sorts of amazing opportunities. Fight the tendency to ask "What if it doesn't work?" and instead ask "What if it does?" What if everything I've ever wanted, needed, and been called to do is on the other side of this powerfully brave decision? If you haven't discovered this already, you will find that many of the best things in life come when we march to the beat of our own drum and stay true to ourselves. When we take that road less traveled that often requires courageous decisions and not always having all the answers, we carve out our own unique path in the world. You were created for such a time as this, so it's time to own it and take that big brave step to conquer your fears.

CHAPTER FIVE

let go

"*Let the morning bring me word of your unfailing love,
for I have put my trust in you.
Show me the way I should go, for to you I entrust my life.*"
Psalm 143:8 (NIV)

BRAVE SURRENDER

What happens if my brave change isn't what I thought it would be?

What happens when things go wrong and I can't let go?

What if it's not the path I chose?

What if part of bravery means patience and stillness on my part?

What if waiting is bravery in disguise?

> When we trust that God knows best for us, we will have the heavenly peace that comes from bravely surrendering to His best for us.

LET GO

One early September in the Nebraska heat, I was sitting in the doctor's office a whopping thirty-seven-and-a-half weeks pregnant with a baby who I was sure was already over ten pounds. I mean it was, after all, my fourth baby, and I knew that this being inside of me was not small. I had been waddling around for weeks feeling certain that I would burst at any moment. Even my sisters' eyes grew wide when they saw my larger-than-life belly. To say I was "not cute" when pregnant was an understatement.

The door to the exam room opened and my always smiling OBGYN walked in with the final hospital registration paperwork for my scheduled C-section in just four days. "Sign here, and you'll be all set to deliver this big boy!" (Yes, we knew it was our fourth boy we were anxiously awaiting.)

I hesitated for a second mulling over something in my head that I wasn't sure I wanted to say out loud, but then I blurted it out. "I want to deliver at a different hospital so that you can tie my tubes after delivery."

I let out a big sigh, and my thoughts raced erratically as I sat there in disbelief. I had never wanted to do something so permanent, but after three C-sections plus the one scheduled in a few days, I suppose you could say I caved to the pressure. I am embarrassed to even admit that. When you have three little boys all under the age of six running around and one on the way, there are no shortages of opinions on parenting, bedtime, discipline, getting them to eat, and when, where, and how to school them. You name it, it was suggested. I learned to let most of it roll right on past me, but the constant comments about the dangers of multiple C-sections stuck with me. Of course, it didn't help that I could be called the "Google

Queen" as I searched up way too many "what if" scenarios. So, in spite of my desire for a very large family, and even though my heart was not at peace at all about the decision to have my tubes tied, cut, and burned, my husband and I decided it made sense for me to have this procedure done. After all, I would already be laying there cut open on the operating table.

I felt a pit in my stomach as my swollen feet carried me out of the office that day. I wasn't at peace, but I was oh-so-ready to get this baby out and have him in my arms. Four days later, as they pulled my 10-pound-13-ounce baby boy out, my heart was overjoyed to hear his cries and see his cute chubby little rolls. As my doctor started the tubal ligation procedure, I didn't stop him.

Later that day, the doctor walked into my room as my sweet little Owen slept in the crook of my arm. The doctor looked right at me and said, "Everything went great and, my goodness, your uterus looked so good you could have kept having kids! I have seen women with more scar tissue after one C-section let alone as many as you've had!"

I will never forget how in that moment I had that final bit of confirmation I had been ignoring. I had made a grave mistake. A permanent mistake. It didn't matter that others had "suggested" that I not risk my life for more babies. I had heard straight from my doctor that, for me, I was relatively safe to continue. Of course, I knew the statistics and medical risks, which are very real, but hearing my doctor say that he would have been comfortable with my choice to have another baby just made this whole thing surreal for me. I had read once in a pregnancy book that a woman should never drastically alter her hairstyle while pregnant because she's not always thinking rationally. But here I had been, four days away from delivering a baby the size of most four-month-old babies, and I had made a permanent fertility decision.

The gravity of my decision stayed with me during those early postpartum weeks. So much so, that when I showed up for my six-week checkup, I cheerfully and confidently told my doctor that I was going to "just start praying that my tubes would grow back together." He smiled a bit and laughed as if he thought I was somehow joking. He proceeded to give me a detailed explanation filled with medical jargon that would make other nonscience nerd types zone out. However, to me, it was fascinating to hear about how he cut the tubes and completely burned them off so that, in his medical mind, there was no hope of them ever repairing themselves. I could see how proud he was that gone were the days of tubes simply "untying" themselves and women conceiving after their tubes were tied. He assured me that in thirty years of practice, no one in the whole clinic had ever had a patient experience a spontaneous reversal of this procedure.

Honestly, in that moment, I should have felt hopeless. I don't know why I didn't. It's not that I was convinced that it would happen, it's just that I believed it could. In the depths of my being, I simply knew that something was missing. I left the office that day with the resolve to pray. Hard. I knew my God could move mountains. I knew the stories of miracles and healing. I was going to pray for healing and a miracle for me.

Sometimes when I tell this story, people ask me if I felt like something was missing because I didn't have a girl. The truth is that I was never lacking by not having a daughter. After four boys, I was convinced we only made boys. It never crossed my mind that a fifth child would be anything but a boy. It's not that I wouldn't be excited about a girl. I just wanted another human to love, raise, and call our own. I went through the next several years of my life praying that God would heal me and perform a miracle in my life to allow us to have another baby.

Here's the thing. I didn't spend my days sad and upset about this missing piece or seemingly unanswered prayer. I was thrilled to be raising my four little boys. We spent months on end at baseball fields, watched the boys play on the playset in the backyard, put in a pool, and took our first of many family vacations in 2011. We were doing life, living life, and loving life, but still…I prayed. I prayed daily for healing and my miracle.

In September 2013, exactly six long years after I began praying for my miracle, I started a new job teaching high school about thirty-five minutes from my house. As an extrovert, I tend to fill car commutes with phone calls and conversations, but at six o'clock in the morning that wasn't an option. I found myself with time to pray on my commute, and I did some soul searching. I felt convicted to change something about the way I was addressing the Lord about my request. I added what I call a "clause" to the prayer. At the end of my prayer for healing and a miracle baby I added a "but"—"But, Lord, if a baby is not your will for my life, please take this desire away so that *I* want what *you* want for me."

In six years, I had never once asked the Lord what He wanted for me. Honestly, I admit that I didn't want to know. I wanted a baby. Now I was at a place of surrender and had come to the realization that if God would take my desire away for a baby, then I wouldn't be sad anymore. You can't be sad about something you don't want, right?

Is there something in your life that you're fervently wanting, praying for, hoping for, but you've never asked God if that's what He wants for you? Does it seem kind of scary to consider that maybe the answer is a "no" or a "not right now"? I would encourage you to search your soul about your wants and desires and how they align with the Lord's direction. What does that look like?

Every day, as I commuted to my job and prayed for my family and extended family to come to know the Lord, for safety and health for those I love, for God to equip me as a wife and mother, and all the other things I prayed for daily, I prayed the new version of my miracle prayer. "Lord, please heal my tubes and allow me to conceive a miracle baby, but if a baby is not your will for my life, please take this desire away so that *I want* what *you want* for me." I prayed this daily for the entire school year. Nine months.

In May 2014, when school finished for the year, we took our boys (ages twelve, ten, nine, and six-and-a-half) on yet another incredible trip to Florida. The trip was so good for the soul. We ate too much good food and soaked up the sun for days. One afternoon as my husband and I sat in the blazing sun next to the pool where our boys wrestled, splashed, and played Marco Polo, I felt joy radiate from within. I felt peace. I felt so content. I looked at my husband and said, "You know what? I want you to know that if someone leaves a baby in a basket on our porch, I still want it." (Okay, side note, that may not be funny to anyone else, but it had kind of been a joke of ours. I wanted a baby so much that I just wished someone would give me one if that's what it took!) However, I needed to make sure that Brent knew exactly how I felt now. I continued, "But…I am finally at a place where God has given me peace. If His answer is 'no' to repairing my tubes and granting us a miraculous conception, then I am good with that. I am at a place where if that's not God's will for our life, I trust that. I am so happy to be at this stage with our boys."

Three days after returning to Nebraska from that trip, I found out I was pregnant. Did you read that? I found out I was pregnant! During vacation, I had felt a little yucky but attributed most of that to the junky food we had been enjoying at Disney and our favorite restaurants. Funnel cakes and ice cream, anyone? I had been eating well all spring, exercising, and had lost about twenty-five pounds, so I assumed that was why my menstrual cycle was messed up. I had talked to my sisters while on vacation and one suggested I at least take a pregnancy test when I returned. Pregnancy was not on my radar since it had been six-and-a-half years since the doctor had tied, cut, and burned my tubes.

I joked and said, "I don't want to spend $10 on a test because it'll be a 'no,' and I don't want to waste $10."

My sister laughed and brought me up to speed on the apparent accuracy of Dollar Store tests. I made a mental note that if I saw a Dollar Store at some point, I would grab a test. Well, what do you know, on the Monday following vacation, as I left the parking lot of our local university where I was working on my master's degree, right in front of me stood a Dollar Store. I sheepishly walked in and hustled to that aisle, the one I hadn't visited in a long time. As I checked out, I silently wondered if the cashier was sizing me up or contemplating my situation.

Thirty minutes later, I arrived home to our remote acreage, and I put the test down on the counter. I cleaned up some things and decompressed for a few minutes while waiting for Brent and the boys. My mind wandered back to the test, so I opened it and realized that it wasn't the pee on the stick kind. It was a "find somewhere to pee, insert a dropper thing, drop a few drops onto a test, and then wait" kind of test. I guess that's what you get for a dollar. I grabbed a red rooster coffee cup from the kitchen. Yep, didn't have a plastic cup. I followed the directions to a T. I planned to wait the recommended ten minutes before looking, but within a split second, I saw it.

Two bright pink lines.

Then I lost it.

I was pregnant.

What. Was. Happening?

My thoughts went something like "Oh my gosh, this test is broken! What is wrong with me? Oh my gosh, I am pregnant! Oh dear. I have to have a C-section! Oh my goodness, how did this happen?"

I started crying hysterically and called my sister who lived across the country. I was so hysterical she could hardly understand me. She panicked thinking someone had died! I finally gasped out the words "Are…these…tests…accurate?…I am hanging up and sending you a picture!"

Thirty seconds later she called me back and said, "You're 1,000 percent pregnant!"

I hung up, took six steps to my bedroom, and fell to my knees on the floor by my bed. I cried out to God saying, "I will never ever again doubt you! You've heard my prayer! Thank you, Jesus, for this miracle!"

At that exact moment, Brent and the boys showed up. People who know me know that I am a calm mom who rarely raises her voice. That all went out the window the second they walked into the kitchen.

"Everyone," I hollered, "GET TO THE BASEMENT!"

I was still crying hysterically as I pointed in the direction of the stairs. The boys didn't say one word as they quickly shuffled to the basement.

I grabbed Brent's arm and pulled him to the bathroom. I pointed at the test on the counter. It took him at least sixty seconds, sixty long, drawn-out seconds, to understand what he was even looking at. Then the excitement and disbelief registered as he said with a huge grin, "You're pregnant!"

At this point, real panic started setting in. Like that true panic attack feeling that you might be familiar with. I felt my heart rate speed up, and fight or flight took over. I grabbed his hand and said repeatedly, "We have to go. We have to go!"

"Where? Where are we going?"

"More tests." I panted out the words. "I need more tests."

We quickly drove eight miles to the nearest store, bought every single pregnancy test on the shelf, and proceeded to dip every single one into the pee-filled rooster mug in our bathroom. We watched each test turn the brightest shade of pink known to man.

I was pregnant.

Undeniably pregnant.

After three pregnancy losses—two before my firstborn and Owen's twin that we lost in the first trimester—I am normally one to keep things hush-hush. However, this situation was totally different. I shoved a handful of positive pregnancy tests into my sweatshirt pocket, and we drove straight to my parents' house. I walked into the kitchen and, without saying a word, reached into my pocket and dumped the whole pile of tests on the counter.

My mom stared, looked at my bloodshot teary eyes, and said, "What are these?"

"You mean they didn't have these in the seventies? These are pregnancy tests! I am pregnant!"

She was equally shocked.

I spent the next couple of hours calling a few friends. It was out of character for me to be so open, but I needed the support. Somehow, saying it out loud a few more times made it more real. Everyone close to me knew this had been the desire of my heart and this was a huge answer to prayer.

A few hours later, the shock wore off, and I started thinking rationally. I realized I might need to go to the hospital as soon as possible. I was no stranger to pregnancy complications, and my geeky fascination with all things medical meant that not only was I aware of randomly rare medical anomalies, but I also knew the dangerous risks of an ectopic pregnancy. I knew that my tubes had been tied. Yet, I also knew definitively after taking seventeen pregnancy tests that I was, in fact, pregnant. I knew there was a chance that this baby was stuck in a tube (or what would likely be a fragment of a removed tube) which could be a recipe for medical disaster especially thirty-five minutes from the nearest hospital. I knew I wouldn't be sleeping at all, so, after the boys went to bed, my friend Sarah drove me to the hospital.

Later that night, I had my confirmation. Against all odds and all medical knowledge and possibilities, a baby was in my uterus, not somewhere unsafe. I was pregnant. With a real baby. Pinch me. I was seven weeks along with a baby that never should have been. Within two days, debilitating nausea set in, but I welcomed every dry heave and trip to the bathroom as a reminder that I was carrying a wonderful miracle inside of me. It's almost as if the awareness of pregnancy brought on all the familiar symptoms, but looking back at the few weeks prior, I could see all the pregnancy signs I had missed because I simply wasn't entertaining the possibility of being pregnant.

I proceeded cautiously with my feelings and excitement, as I, and other women with a history of recurrent pregnancy loss, often do. Why is it that sometimes we cope by worrying about the worst? It's not like worrying about miscarriage ever actually made it hurt less when it happened. I didn't want to get too excited in case I would lose the baby, but a part of me didn't think there was any chance that God would answer our prayer only to take our baby away. I knew that I could choose to spend every day of the first trimester riddled with anxiety, and it wouldn't make it less painful if I would need to say goodbye.

When I went for my official doctor's visit, I got to record our little one's super strong heartbeat on my cell phone. The rhythmic thumping was like a sweet melody that I could not get enough of. My doctor decided to watch me closely considering the unexpected nature of my pregnancy. I welcomed the extra attention and particularly loved the extra ultrasounds to see my miracle.

Then, my world crashed down. As I neared the very end of the first trimester, I heard the silence. The lack of the fluttering heartbeat on the ultrasound. Before the sonographer even had a chance to say the words, I knew. It was over. Our miracle baby's heart had stopped beating. I crumbled. I cried. And then I texted my friends and family one by one before I headed home.

I had actually started the process of notifying everyone by calling my dad first. But, hearing him cry and break in pain over this loss confirmed that everyone else needed a text because I couldn't bear to hear anyone else's heart break along with mine. My friends and family grieved with me.

I drove the twenty-five minutes home, and I prayed. I prayed as tears poured out of my eyes. You want to know what I didn't do? I didn't get angry. My lack of anger has perplexed so many people, and many ask how I didn't get angry and ask God "Why? Why would you answer my prayer after almost seven years and then take my miracle away?" Honestly, I didn't think that way at all. I prayed prayers of gratitude in that moment. I was so grateful that God had given me a sweet baby to love and take care of within my body even though the time was brief.

I believed in my heart of hearts that this little one was a girl, so we named her Faith. I listened over and over to a Jeremy Camp song that talks about walking by faith even when we cannot see and how the broken road we are on prepares God's will for us. In that moment, I clung to those words. I chose to walk by faith even though I did not understand why it was working out this way. Every time I hear that song, I think of my baby Faith. God chose me for a brief season to hold Faith inside my womb. He let us love her, pray for her, and dream big dreams about what might have been for her.

During this time, God taught me the most powerful lesson of my life. For years and years, I prayed for what I wanted. I prayed for the baby that I wanted. At times, I felt broken and desperate, but as soon as I added my "clause," my "oh so powerful afterthought," I was able to fully experience God's work on my heart. He truly molded my desires and transformed my will into His. He brought me to a place of brave surrender. He drew me to a state of complete peace with His plan. And then He showed me a miracle.

Even through the loss of Faith, I never experienced anger or doubt about God's goodness. Of course, I experienced the loss and grief that losing an unborn child brings. The sorrow was crushing and took my breath away at times. Leaving the operating room after my D&C, I sobbed uncontrollably knowing my miracle baby was no longer in my body. Not being angry at God does not mean I didn't care. Quite the contrary. A piece of my heart was taken that day when I lost our little Faith. While I don't understand why we lost her, I do understand that God's plan and His ways have been and always will be higher than mine. I trust that there is a huge divine plan, and I don't have to understand it to believe it.

In my total surrender, I allowed God to show me His heart and what He can do. Quite literally, three days after saying out loud that I had accepted God's answer, I found out what His answer really was. How amazing is it that, in the very moment I let go, I was already seven weeks pregnant with Faith? In this instance, He waited for me to let go, so that He could show me His handiwork.

What is that area of your life that you are trying to control? Maybe for you it's a family move or a battle with a teenager or extended family drama or feud that's continued for way too long. What would happen if you chose to let go and let God? What might be in store for you if you chose to ask God to mold your desires to be His desires for your life? We women are, more often than not, creatures of control. We feel at peace and more comfortable when we know what's next and when we feel that we are somehow in charge of it all. This is why brave surrender is so powerful. It's not until we realize that we ultimately have zero control, accept it, and invite God to do His thing that we experience the miracle of walking by faith.

When you let go and truly surrender, a supernatural peace comes over you. It's similar to that feeling you experience when you get something off your chest or a situation works itself out. You sigh with relief and feel surprised when you realize how heavy the burden had weighed on your shoulders. So many times I have dreaded a conversation or had the weight of an upcoming meeting weighing on me. I had no clue how much the weight was affecting me until it was over and I found myself skipping out of the meeting and falling into a deep restful sleep for the first time in weeks. I had failed to see that I was carrying so much or was letting something consume me. Surrendering to God's will is a lot like that feeling of unburdening. You'll find peace and freedom in the act of letting go of control. You will be more "along for the ride," if you will. Doesn't that sound amazing? To be along for the ride of your life and not having to steer the ship every minute of every day?

How do you surrender to God's will? Find at least one area of your life where you've been exceptionally strong-willed. Choose to let go of trying to shape the outcome in the way that you want it. Release that area or that thing to God. Give yourself permission to step back and breathe. Try, this one time, to completely trust that it will work out according to God's plan. Pray that God would shape the desires of your heart to want His will for your situation and ask Him to align what you want with what He wants.

Some of you might be nodding right now because you've identified a situation you need to surrender. Or maybe you're stomping your feet because you know exactly what situation you are grappling to control and are feeling quite uncomfortable at what you know you need to do. But maybe you are one of the ones who is struggling to figure out what situation you need to surrender. If you are having a hard time with this, you might want to try something super brave. You may need to phone a friend and ask her to help you see your blind spots and what that thing might be for you.

Surrender takes patience. You may not see an obvious answer right away. Remember, it took me nine months to get to a place of feeling totally at peace with God's answer being "no." I didn't change my prayer and secretly still hope that God would choose my way. And, honestly, I thought He already had told me "no," and I was essentially asking Him to help me be content inside of the "no." So, it's like the old Garth Brooks song about thanking God for unanswered prayers. I have come to realize that prayers are always answered. Sometimes the best answer is "no" or "not right now." But, when we trust that God knows best for us, we will have the heavenly peace that comes from bravely surrendering to His best for us.

CHAPTER SIX

listen to your gut

"Who has put wisdom in the inward parts
or given understanding to the mind?"
Job 38:36 (ESV)

BRAVE INTUITION

How do I know what choices to make?

Is it okay to walk away from situations that feel wrong?

> You are the one that ultimately lives with the end result of every decision you make. It's okay to not take the path that is predictable.

I was driving down a busy highway in my silver Dodge Grand Caravan when Logan was three, Mason was one-and-a-half, and Parker was just a few months old. Logan and Mason were chatting about their favorite Wiggles episodes while Parker slept comfortably in his rear-facing car seat. Car after car passed us going the other direction. I am sure most were heading toward town to get groceries or have a day of fun while we were heading further and further into the country toward our peaceful acreage. All of a sudden, a random thought popped into my head. "If I were to reach for something and accidentally swerve and hit a semi head-on, what would people think happened to us? Would we all die instantly?" As soon as that thought popped into my head, I was completely mortified! Where on earth had it come from? I had never thought anything like that in my life. That thought was just one of the dozens of disturbing things that had been happening since Parker's birth.

I couldn't quite figure out why these thoughts interrupted my previously "normal" existence. When Parker was just a week old, I had felt weepier than I had remembered after my first two deliveries. But, honestly, since Mason, my second baby, had spent time so much time in the NICU and had so many obstacles to overcome in those early weeks, I was actually on cloud nine that Parker came home the same day I did. He was perfectly healthy, and it was such a welcome change not dealing with all the preemie stuff this time around. I didn't feel depressed either, and I didn't feel particularly sad. Sure, I was a bit overwhelmed caring for three little boys ages three and under while my husband worked seventy-five hours a week in our landscaping company. However, I assumed I'd get through the crazy days soon enough.

But I still had an uneasy feeling about the weird things happening since Parker's birth. One time, when I walked down the stairs with Parker in my arms, I had an intrusive thought about what would happen if I tripped and Parker's head hit the angled wooden railing just right. I panicked and grew scared of carrying him down the steps for fear that something would actually happen. Every time I did carry him down, I covered the top of his head so that I didn't accidentally bump him. Another time I opened the sliding glass door while holding him and walked out onto our second-story deck. Just then I pictured myself tripping on one of the boards and my sweet baby flying over the edge of the deck to the concrete below. While accidentally hurting my baby terrified me, I had no basis for these fears.

Everywhere I turned, it seemed like some new worry showed up out of nowhere. They were always random, extremely unlikely to actually ever happen, and not consistent with anything I had ever worried about before. As I became more and more fearful, I quit walking down the stairs with Parker and going out on the deck with him so I didn't have to worry about hurting him.

My gut told me something just was not right about everything going on. I had always had the normal, protective mom feelings after my babies were born. I wanted to fiercely protect them as any mom would. I wanted to guard them, take care of them, and make sure they were safe and well-nourished. I never had these random thoughts that were so out of character and so opposite of the person I am. (Honestly, I didn't feel that I was a threat to Parker or his brothers. These thoughts were more about hoping something didn't happen to him.) And I had never struggled with depression in my life. Sure, I had my fair share of anxiety, fear of flying, and other worries occasionally, but nothing as disturbing as what I noticed after Parker's birth.

I didn't have a lot of friends who were moms yet, so I didn't quite know whom to turn to. I didn't say too much to my husband for fear that he wouldn't understand. How could he understand when I didn't understand myself? He did know that evenings were a bit rough for me. I found myself getting particularly emotional in the evenings, and in general, I felt my fears and racing thoughts increase in the evening only to be slightly less by the time the sun came up.

Finally, I decided to go talk to my doctor, and I am so glad I did. He immediately knew that I was suffering from postpartum anxiety. I won't get into the ins and outs of the medical reasons for postpartum anxiety, but hormones and lots of body changes can certainly play a huge part. Statistics show that 10–15 percent of women suffer from some sort of postpartum mood disorder, including postpartum depression (PPD), postpartum anxiety/OCD, and postpartum psychosis. That 10–15 percent stat reflects those who doctors diagnose; the real number could be quite a bit higher.

After a few months on a low dose of anti-anxiety medication, I was able to wean off and never had a recurrence of postpartum anxiety after pregnancy again. I felt like a completely new person after I started the medication. While it was a bit scary and slightly embarrassing to tell my doctor the kinds of things I was thinking (and it feels awkward sharing those thoughts here), it was a relief to have an answer.

Growing up, I spent most of my life stuffing my thoughts, feelings, and emotions. I believed that what I felt and what I needed didn't matter. As an adult, I realized life wasn't supposed to be that way, and I challenged myself to do brave things and express myself. When I sensed my gut telling me something was just not right, I knew I needed to figure out what was going on, even if it meant sharing my personal thoughts with someone.

It's important as women that we give ourselves permission to trust our intuition. Sometimes intuition is that gut feeling we get, like when I knew something just wasn't right with my thoughts about Parker. For us Christians, that gut feeling is often the Holy Spirit nudging us in a certain direction. Other times our "mother's instinct," what we moms somehow develop through the process of becoming mothers, lets us know that something is "off" with our child or our pregnancy.

Trusting your intuition can be scary because it often means choosing a path that doesn't look obvious to those around us. Everyone else may have a strong opinion about your relationship, your career, your geographical location, or your child-rearing skills, but you are the one right smack dab in the middle of it all. You are the one who can pray for guidance, direction, and peace about big, bold decisions. You are the one that ultimately lives with the end result of every decision you make. It's okay to not take the path that is predictable. It's okay not to follow in the footsteps of someone else in your family who believes their way is *the* way.

At the beginning of this chapter is a verse from the Book of Job. Do you remember Job's story? If you're not familiar with Job, his story is in the Bible's Old Testament, but here's the really short version. He was a wealthy man who had a wonderful family and a thriving farm with livestock and crops. He was well-regarded in the community too. Then tragedy struck. Thieves stole some of his livestock and killed some servants. On another portion of his land, fire struck and killed the remaining livestock and servants. And then a windstorm demolished the home of his oldest son and killed all ten of Job's children. All on the same day. After all that, his friends provided some unwise counsel, and Job's body broke out in sores. Job's struggle was real, yet he never lost sight of God. He weighed the counsel of his friends against what he knew about God, and he listened to his gut. He knew God had a purpose; he didn't understand that purpose, but he stayed true to who he was. He chose the path that wasn't predictable. And God blessed him.

In a society where we are taught to put ourselves last or where we *choose* to put ourselves last, we need to know that it's not just *okay* to listen to our gut, it's necessary. You have every right to walk away from something that just doesn't feel right anymore. It's okay if sometimes you say, "I need to think about this a little bit more." Job rejected the counsel of his friends and even his wife who had told him to curse God because their advice did not agree with what he knew to be true. If you have something nagging at you in the back of your mind, your intuition is trying to tell you something. Maybe there's another solution to your problem or another option for you.

The choice to follow your intuition is not easy. Making the hard decisions and trusting your gut, even when it's the opposite of advice given to you, is difficult. I tend to be a people pleaser. I want others to think I'm making the right choice. I want others to be in agreement with my decisions and to think I am doing a good job. But at the end of the day, I need to make my decisions based on my God-given intuition, and I need to stop the things that God has called me to stop. I need to work where God has called me to go, and I need to have relationships and serve in the way that God has called me to do, not what everyone else thinks I should do.

You can make the hard choices too. Pay attention to the times when you aren't feeling certainty in your life and be brave enough to make the right choice even when it's not the obvious choice to everyone around you. If something is keeping you up at night, I encourage you to pray about whatever it is. If God lays someone on your heart, pray for that person because you don't know what might be happening in her life and the reason that God has laid her on your heart.

CHAPTER SEVEN
stay the course

"I can do all things through him who strengthens me."
Philippians 4:13 (ESV)

BRAVE COMMITMENT

What if I feel like giving up?

I set my goals, but now they seem impossible—what do I do?

> Being committed means staying the course even on days when you don't feel like it.

ONLY A COUPLE OF MONTHS into our marriage, while we were still in our honeymoon phase, Brent and I had a serious talk over dinner one night. We were barely twenty-three years old at the time and had no idea that the next several years would involve us practically growing up while married. During our conversation, we talked about "forever." You see, our upbringings were vastly different. I was a child of divorce who had weathered a couple of different custody battles before the age of fifteen while Brent's parents had stayed married until his dad's death at age forty-five when Brent was sixteen years old. I wanted so much to have a marriage that would last until "death do us part."

As a Christian, I knew what the Bible said about the covenant of marriage, and we talked a lot about what the Bible said and what it meant for us. Even though I knew I was loved, I had a little bit of an uneasy feeling in the pit of my stomach. I believed that it was important to commit through thick and thin and that divorce should be a rarity, but I had seen more examples in my immediate and extended family of people leaving when things didn't work out than of people staying. I had also seen others in my life who I knew were not happy but they stayed married because they were "supposed to." I didn't want to stay married because we were "supposed to."

That night, I said to Brent, "I don't want to settle for just a mediocre marriage. I don't want to stay married only because the Bible says to. I want to stay married because we create a loving, committed, and fulfilling relationship. I want to choose each other every single day. I don't want to wake up twenty-five years into our marriage when our kids have grown up and moved out only to look at each other and say 'who are you? I don't even know you anymore.'" I had no plans to be a divorce statistic, but complacency terrified me. I had watched couples in my life who truly drifted apart over the years. By the time they were in their forties and fifties, they didn't have anything in common anymore. For all those couples, it seemed like the thing to do was throw in the towel and find someone else with common interests. I didn't want that. The thought of simply coexisting with my husband made me feel sick. I guess you can say I'm wired for connection.

I know it seems kind of silly that we talked about this subject so early in our marriage, but I think that speaks to my overachieving, perfectionistic nature. Every now and again it serves me well. I can be quite all or nothing when it comes to making a decision. I'm either all in or all out. I also tend to be a planner and a strategist. So, from the very beginning of our marriage, I found myself wanting to be in a proactive mode rather than a reactive mode. In order to be proactive, Brent and I knew we had to stay committed to our relationship and to making it stronger each day.

I've read before that the definition of commitment is "Doing the thing that you said you were going to do long after the feeling that you had when you said it has gone." Being committed means staying the course even on days when you don't feel like it. Being committed to the gym means going even when it's snowing outside or you're too tired after work. Being committed to the new business you started means making the phone calls and finishing the projects even when your favorite reality TV show comes on. Being committed to your new health plan means meal prep and planning even when you're exhausted after putting the kids to bed. Commitment requires a determination to keep going even when you don't feel like it.

My husband and I have been together for over twenty years, and I can tell you we've weathered a lot of ups and downs. We've had months and years where we were at the highest of highs and commitment was easy. But we've also had seasons that weren't so easy when we seemed to drift apart and sometimes felt like we were closer to our friends than to each other. There were even seasons when we felt totally alone but were unsure what to do about it.

The year 2010 was a particularly rough year for us. A lot of things happened that I think set us up for a rough year. The years leading up to 2010 were pretty good but busy. Our four boys were younger back then, and having them so close in age was more exhausting than we could've ever imagined. I have no regrets about having four boys under the age of six at a certain point in time, but looking back I do wonder how we got through it on zero sleep.

On one of those busy days, I was downstairs folding laundry just like any other day. The sun was shining through the window, and I stood there in a white T-shirt and yoga pants. Out of the corner of my eye, I could see the boys through the window playing outside as I carefully folded each bath towel into thirds. I am sure the exhaustion that a mom of littles feels every single day probably led to the fact that I was feeling more emotional than usual. Lost in thought, I allowed my mind to wander. This memory is burned in my mind because I remember *exactly* how I *felt*.

Brent and I weren't in a fight and hadn't even had a recent conversation, but something was wrong inside of me. My mind raced with all sorts of thoughts, and I felt rather disconnected from him. I was running in one direction building a home-based business and trying to get through the day with little boys. At the same time, his landscape business was growing, but the long hours meant that there wasn't a lot of time for deep conversation or getting out of the house to have fun. We had not been prioritizing quality time, and truth be told, we both were getting our fulfillment through parenting and our respective business adventures and not each other.

When Brent came downstairs a short time later, I asked him, "Are you *in love* with me or do you simply *love* me because you're supposed to? Do you love me because I'm the mother of your children, and we've been together so long you don't know any different?"

He looked at me dumbfounded. His expression should've been my first clue that he hadn't let his mind go down the road of wondering about where we stood ten years into this marriage thing. Of course, he reassured me of how much he loved me, but my mind wasn't at peace. Our conversation didn't go much further at this point. He assumed the conversation was over, and the boys came in ready for dinner.

Looking back, I can see some of the signs that led up to my feelings of discontentment and confusion. I was building a home-based business as a representative in a multi-level marketing company. I was actually good at it! I created a significant income for our family on my schedule. And I found out I was good at teaching men and women how to build a business, stick it out through the tough stuff, and develop strategies that taught even the most brand new person how to successfully build a business. I was confident in the model of network marketing and that women specifically could build a business from home. Plus, I was traveling a bit and spending a lot of time on stage training others. I never thought that the shy quiet girl from elementary school would morph into a confident presenter and trainer.

One of the things that was interesting to see was how admired I was by other people in my company. When you achieve the level of success that I did, as weird as it sounds, you become a little bit of a celebrity within your company. I know that seems kind of crazy, but people look up to those who have achieved what they are longing to achieve. People often sought me out as a top leader for advice on how to build their business, and I spent lots of time in conversations with other independent representatives talking about business and life. The attention was a little awkward, but it felt so good to be needed and valued.

Sometimes, driving home from meetings I found my mind telling me how much more others appreciated me than those in my own home did. I started wondering if Brent *did* value what I was doing. At trainings and in conversations, men would say, "Wow, you are so driven!" or "Wow, I bet your husband must be so proud of you!" or "Your husband is so lucky to have a wife that can do what you do!" I would smile graciously, and you would think I would have been flattered, but honestly, it just made me look at my own situation and start to have doubts. It made me wonder if Brent was actually proud of me. I knew he supported me in my business, and he showed this by caring for the kids without complaint when I was running around holding meetings and events. But I think my heart was just longing for more. He's a man of few words, so although I should have *assumed* that he was proud of me because he didn't tell me he *wasn't*, he didn't often tell me that he was.

We've all been in the position where we feel like our hard work goes unnoticed. Maybe it's at work, maybe as a mom, or maybe around the house. Our human nature needs that assurance that we

Don't stare at everything that's wrong.

Be grateful for what is right.

are being noticed and appreciated. I'm sure Brent likely felt the same way. I tried to stay in the habit of telling him thank you for working so hard, but I know I could have done better showing him just how much I noticed what he did for our family. When you're up to your eyeballs in kids, work, and so many things to do around the house, it's often easy to let days go by without showing gratitude or without recognizing someone's efforts. I think I had some subtle resentment building for a couple of years. I was overwhelmed with my role of being a wife and mother and bringing in an income, and I spent too much time focusing on what was *missing* in my marriage than focusing on what was going *right*.

I also know that motherhood can be very lonely. It seems like a paradox that being surrounded by little ones all day long could be lonely, but without adult conversation, many moms feel lonely just like I did. Sure, we have playdates and, of course, now we have social media mom's groups, but there is still an undertone of loneliness. I know the loneliness had a lot to do with my feelings of longing for something more. I craved lengthy conversations with my husband. I wanted to talk about my latest weight loss endeavors or to share what was new in my business, but by the time he came home from work, we didn't have a lot of time for chitchat.

There's a saying that says, "You steer where you stare." I was staring at everything that was wrong rather than being grateful for what was right. I was watching the water pour into the boat, rather than patching the holes. My focus led to a lot of discontentment. I even started believing the lie that my husband would be happier with someone else more like him, and I would be happier with someone just like me. I had myself convinced that our personalities were so different and that we had drifted apart when, in reality, I had taken my eyes off of what was most important. I compared us to couples on TV and other couples that *seemed* to have everything that we didn't. (I stress *seemed* because I know that what we portray outwardly isn't always the full picture, and we often share the highlight reel of our lives with those around us.)

Over and over, I discovered that you find exactly what you're looking for. After a rocky few months full of confusion and lots of deep conversations with my husband, I made a *choice* to do a complete one-eighty. I emphasize *choice* here because it's not like some crazy, giddy made-for-tv romance washed over me. Truth be told, I was still feeling kind of "blah" and distant from my husband. I wasn't feeling a spark or a super deep connection. However, I made a choice to turn my thinking around. I made a choice to stop staring at things that only served to foster resentment and uncertainty. I renewed my commitment to work through our marriage and, once again, not settle for mediocre. I refused to use the excuse that we had kids and were too busy for time with each other. We had been putting off installing an in-ground pool in our backyard. We kept saying that we would do it someday. That summer we decided to quit "someday-ing" our plan and do it now. We knew the pool would be an incredible investment in our family and would allow us to spend some much-needed time together. We made time for *us* again.

Looking back now, I am astounded that the second ten years of our marriage have been ten times more rewarding than the first ten years (and the majority of the first ten was pretty darn good!). The turning point of 2010 in our minds and hearts dramatically changed the course of where Brent and I are today. I can see the ways that

God honored our commitment to working through the tough seasons rather than bailing during the storm. However, just because we didn't bail out doesn't mean I don't think there are ever legitimate reasons that couples need to divorce. In our situation, we chose to grow and change, and it did take some change on both of our parts, but that effort and change were worth it to be where we're at today.

About three years into our marriage, a good friend told me that love is a choice. She said, "The feelings sometimes fade. That warm fuzzy feeling when he looks at you across the room may not always be there, but we have the ability to choose each day if we are going to love." If we had made a different decision in 2010, if we had thrown up our hands and said, "You know what? We gave it a good run, but maybe something else would be better," we wouldn't have ever met our sweet Hazel, our daughter born in 2015 and truly a miracle. God has reminded us over and over that He is faithful and that the feelings will follow when we choose love and choose each other every day.

When people ask me how to stay committed or how to keep from giving up, I often reply by saying "Remove from yourself the option to quit." I know that sounds basic, but that's really what commitment is about. When I'm training on stage talking about what it looks like to build a six- or seven-figure income in network marketing/social marketing, I say the same thing—finish what you start. If from day one you say to yourself "I will not quit building my business," then your only option is success. If you commit to writing a book and say, "No ifs, ands, or buts about it, I will get the book done!" then you will complete the book. When the options of quitting, leaving, or stopping are off the table, your only option left is commitment.

In my weight loss journey, the philosophy of refusing to quit is what has pushed me through. I had complained about my weight for years and made every excuse I could about why I wasn't losing weight. I was very aware that I was eating too much of the wrong things, but there was always a holiday trip or a visit from friends or family that somehow gave me a reason for not sticking to my plan. I would lose five or ten pounds, get derailed by my lack of commitment, and then start again, quit again, start again, and quit again. The cycle was vicious. When I finally reached a place where I was ready to commit once and for all, I removed from myself the option to quit. I needed a complete mindset shift, so I used daily positive affirmations. I told myself every day that quitting was not an option. This time *would* be different. Vacations, company staying with us, holidays, and birthdays would always be a part of the journey, but they were not a reason to *stop* the journey. I've had bumps in the road but no roadblocks that have kept me from continuing on my quest for health.

What is that thing in your life that requires your commitment? What is one area that maybe you have one foot out the door so that you're not really "all in"? What is a goal that you have set that you're still thinking about and working toward but stagnant in your progress? Is there a project at your house? Something with your health? Do you have a relationship that needs full commitment, but you're just not doing it?

First, take quitting off the table. Don't allow it to be an option for you. With quitting off the table, what is your option? Your only option is to complete the project. Now you can get counseling or work through the relationship. Now you are free to hit that next business goal. If you've thrown away the option to quit, you can make that big move. You can make the big change. With quitting not in the cards for you anymore, success and achievement are your only options.

Second, stay *committed* to your decision, but be *flexible* in the "how-to." My decision to be 1,000 percent *all in* in my marriage meant that we needed some new approaches and new strategies. I knew that the definition of insanity was doing the same thing over and over again and expecting a different result. So, I needed to stay flexible in the "how-to" or flexible in our approach. This meant addressing uncomfortable conversations head-on rather than stuffing my emotions as I had before. This meant accepting certain parts of my husband and letting go of trying to change them. On my husband's side of the equation, it meant talking more and having deeper conversations than we had in the past. He vowed to spend more quality time together even if it meant just listening to me ramble about things. Our new approach meant *committing* to a date night rather than *hoping* that maybe it would happen. Our flexibility in creating our dream marriage was exciting!

In business, part of staying flexible in the "how-to" means maybe "adjusting the sails" a little bit. If what you're doing is not working, but you've committed to the end result, you may need to adjust your methods. Can you achieve the same goal but find a different way to get there? If you're committed to your business goal, it may be time to listen to a new podcast, seek out an accountability partner, or find a new method of achieving what you set out to do when you said "yes."

When I decided to lose my weight once and for all, I embraced intermittent fasting. In the past, I had used counting calories, counting points, or low carb eating to lose weight. I had read about intermittent fasting before and decided to incorporate it into my weight loss plan. So, I committed to the goal of losing weight and then was flexible in the method to get there. That flexibility made all the difference in achieving my goals. I was stubborn in my commitment and steadfast in the decision I made, but I was open to new ways of getting there.

Third, remind yourself that commitment is not a *word* but an *action*. You say the words "I do" on your wedding day, but your actions show that you *really* do. When you sign up for a home-based business, your words and your signature on the dotted line say "I am doing this!" but it's getting into activity and starting to share the product or service that show the commitment. Your journey toward a healthier you is simply a thought or an idea until you get out and start walking, begin prepping healthy meals, or habitually follow a new way of eating. Putting feet to the words that you say takes you from being *all talk* to *walking the walk*.

It's time to get real about some areas in your life that just aren't worth walking away from. It's time to give your all and be brave as you renew your commitment. Make a promise to yourself that this is the year that you're going *all in*. Make a choice that this is the year that you stop settling for less than you deserve and less than you're capable of. You're going to have to do the hard things to get where you want to go and to accomplish that burning desire in your life. You're going to have to draw a line in the sand and make a firm decision to commit. Just remember that the best things in your life will happen once you commit and don't quit.

CHAPTER EIGHT

seek support

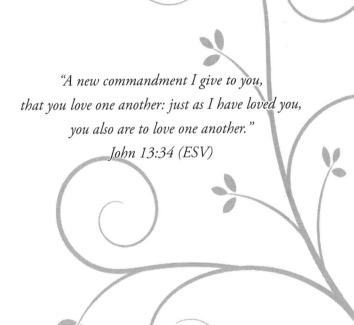

*"A new commandment I give to you,
that you love one another: just as I have loved you,
you also are to love one another."*
John 13:34 (ESV)

BRAVE RELATIONSHIPS

Do you prioritize relationships in your life?

Have your friendships been a two-way street?

Is there someone who has been there for you that you need to step in and offer more support to?

Is there a friend that needs your forgiveness?

> Good friendships are worth searching for if you don't have them; they're worth fighting for if they're broken; and they're worth cultivating when you have them.

SEEK SUPPORT

THE OLDER I GET THE more I realize how important it is to have good friends and solid relationships. Good friendships can be a boost to self-esteem, help us fight loneliness, give us a sense of belonging, and can be the voice of reason when life often seems confusing. Friendships have an impact on our mood, and they help make us better wives and mothers. How? I am a better wife because I am not relying on my husband to meet 100 percent of my conversational and emotional needs. I am a better mother because I have examples of other great mothers in my life. I have people to talk to who have walked where I'm walking and can give advice on those tough parenting situations. Deep relationships give us the support we naturally need when we are going through the toughest of times. You know, those times we all *must* go through, but none of us *want* to go through.

I wholeheartedly believe that we women need to bravely pursue and maintain tight friendships. We must prioritize quality time with friends even if it means talking over the phone with our long-distance friends. And we need to be brave when addressing misunderstandings and not allow unnecessary drama to create wedges in our relationships. True friendship offers unconditional support and loyalty and is full of incredible trust.

My friend Dani and I have weathered countless life storms together. Honestly, we've been through so much I could probably write a book about what a long-term friendship looks like through good times and bad. Our friendship spans well over a decade of major life moments—births and deaths, heartaches, and rejoicing. But, more importantly, it's also made up of simply being there for each other. I need her, and she needs me.

I remember sitting in front of Dani's house in her black SUV one cold Nebraska February day while she tried to figure out how to wrap her brain around her surprise fifth pregnancy, seven years after her fourth and, supposedly final, child had been born. The timing wasn't perfect in her life, but when is the timing ever perfect for having a baby? Emotions overwhelmed her, but she knew her husband and four kids would be thrilled. I'll never forget weeks later being with her whole family crammed into a small ultrasound room and finding out that baby number five would be their fourth girl! I cried my eyes out in the delivery room as I watched her deliver one of the most beautiful baby girls I have ever laid eyes on in my life.

A few years later, I cried my eyes out again when Dani and her family moved out of state. I knew stopping by on a random Wednesday to visit would no longer be our reality. Distance changed the frequency with which we hung out, but it didn't change our hearts. One October morning Dani called to say her mom was very sick. The doctors had asked Dani to quickly fly to Nebraska because the situation wasn't good. As an only child, Dani didn't have the comfort of siblings to walk this journey with, and we all know no instruction manual explains how to prepare for and cope with the loss of a parent. I met Dani at the hospital, and my heart broke as I watched her heart break. She had told me for years that she had promised her mom that when the time came for her to meet Jesus that she would "sing her into glory" so she would not be alone. That night in that hospital room, I watched Dani lay her head on her mom and heard her sing a cappella some of the most beautiful worship songs I had ever heard. I could not take Dani's pain away, but I could be right beside her. I rested my hand on her back so that she knew that I was there walking through the valley with her. Dani's angelic voice carried out the door and through the hallways as she praised Jesus and sang her mama home to heaven. The beauty and emotion of the moment moved the nurses to tears. Later, I stayed with Dani and watched as she memorized everything about her mom before they took her body away.

My dear friend Ashley and her young son stayed with us for an entire summer as she worked through the loneliness of separation and divorce. That summer was a time of incredible growth for Ashley as she read books about healing and moving on. She worked through some tough issues from her past, and we spent hours and hours talking through her feelings. Those months were not easy for her, but I chose to stand in the gap with her and simply be that friend that was nearby whenever she needed me.

A few years later Ashley came to visit from Michigan for a week during the summer. My boys loved it whenever Ashley came to town. Not only did they have a blast playing with her son, but she would rough house with them in the pool and spend time with them. This visit was extra special because it was the first time I had seen Ashley since telling her I was pregnant after seven years of praying for my tubes to heal. While she was visiting, I had a doctor's appointment scheduled to check on our little miracle baby. I already had a recording of her heartbeat on my phone, but I was excited to hear it again. That day, my dreams shattered when I heard the silence. No heartbeat. Our little Faith had died.

After Brent and I left the doctor's office, we went to the local donut shop to try and process our loss over a cream-filled Long John. Brent had to go back to work for the rest of the day, so I headed home by myself. As soon as I entered the house, Ashley wrapped her arms around me and then let me be. She cared for my kids, she answered my calls and texts, she accepted flowers at the door, and she let me sob as I soaked in the bathtub and then laid on my bed all afternoon. Somehow just knowing that Ashley was in the other room taking care of the boys and making dinner gave me immense comfort. When I came home from the D&C the next day and the grief hit me anew as the hormones crashed and a feeling of emptiness overtook me, Ashley was there. Her presence and the obvious help she offered took some of the sting away. Words cannot describe the loneliness a woman feels when she loses the baby inside of her. Ashley had never experienced that kind of loss, but she walked alongside me in my grief. Cling to those friends who can help you through the dark times.

In case you are wondering if I ever do anything fun with my friends or if our friendships are all doom and gloom, let me tell you about how Dani and Ashley helped me lose weight. In January of 2020, I was sick and tired of being overweight and making excuses for myself. After dropping Hazel off at preschool one morning, I texted Ashley and Dani and said I needed an impromptu three-way call with them. Within minutes we were on the phone. I knew they each wanted to lose twenty-five pounds and I was at the place where I needed to lose close to one-hundred pounds. I said "Ladies, it's time. I have to lose this weight once and for all. I know the daily work of eating habits and exercise is on me, but I need you. I need your support and encouragement. Please remind me that I can do this. Please check in with me consistently, and I will do the same. This is our year to get this over with. We all can hit this goal if we work together and hold each other accountable."

Then I told them that if we EACH hit our goal that I would take them on a girls' weekend for us all to celebrate. That created accountability between all of us. We didn't want to let each other down! Week after week and day after day we pushed each other to stay the course. We reminded each other of the end goal. We talked about all the health reasons for continuing to pursue losing weight. When one of us stalled or had a day when we felt like we blew it, we helped each other refocus and recommit. Our daily check-ins were a huge part of all our success on our weight loss journey. It wasn't easy, but we didn't go it alone.

When I was embarking on one of the biggest business adventures of my life, I was excited but stressed at the same time. Paperwork was piled high, self-imposed deadlines were looming, and I was trying to juggle motherhood and fifty other things. Can you relate? When I shared my business idea with Ashley, she hardly let me finish my sentence before she exclaimed, "I am IN, and I don't need to know anymore. I will sell paper plates with you if that's what it is!" While others may think I am crazy or not understand the dreams of an entrepreneur, Ashley and Dani have always been along for the next adventure and offering unconditional support. They know that I don't make rash decisions. They watch me prayerfully consider my options, strategize the process, and listen to what I am called to do. They have watched me hesitate until I have clarity from the Lord, and then they see me bravely take the big leaps of faith. They trust my decisions, but even more than that, they believe in me with their whole hearts. They believe that whatever I set my heart and mind to, I will achieve.

Friends see the best in us and believe the best about us even when we might not see it. Our closest friends typically know our past. They often know our deepest secrets. They usually know the ways we've stumbled, and they love us anyway. They don't judge us based on one snapshot, one decision, or one season of our life. They see the big picture. They will have our best interests at heart, and we will do the same for them. Even though they believe the best about us, they will make sure to warn us when we're on the brink of a bad decision. When we hesitate to take that brave step toward change, commitment, or parenting in our lives, our friends will remind us how powerful and capable we truly are. They'll give us that push we need. They'll remind us to chase our brave. True friends encourage us to be better. They are there to push us when we need it. They encourage us to be our best self.

However, it's easy to fall into the trap of expecting one person or one relationship to meet all our needs. This is especially true in marriage where our spouse is typically the person we are closest to and our best friend. In the previous chapter, I talked about my marriage funk in 2010. During that time, I realized I had been expecting my husband to be "my everything." I had this idealized image—probably from watching too many romantic comedy movies—that Brent could be 100 percent of everything I needed. Because I was stuffing all my feelings, he didn't know he wasn't meeting some of my needs.

With a renewed commitment to thriving in our marriage, I reminded myself—actually, for the first time, admitted to myself—that it was okay if I had girlfriends to rely on for some of the support that I longed for in my life. It was unfair for me to expect Brent to be my everything and to meet my every need, so I analyzed what proper expectations I could place on him because he was committed to meeting more of my needs and to stepping up in his role. I asked what things I could do to better show *him* love and be a better wife for *him*. I knew I had plenty of room for improvement. I started focusing on all the things I was *grateful* for in my marriage. I trusted that by choosing to love him, all the feelings I had lost or stuffed away would follow. We got better at talking through the tough things, and we both quit assuming what the other meant or felt. We started asking more questions and sought to understand each other.

I started to consistently remind myself (and I still do) that I have a loyal, devoted husband who would literally work at a fast-food restaurant overnight if that meant providing for his family. I have a husband who collaborates with me and lets me chase after my big, bold, brave ideas. He has been with me through thick and thin and during the trials of our pregnancies. He has been the rock of our life together. He may not be as conversational as I thought I needed, and I usually need to give him time to process rather than expect instant answers. He may not be as outgoing as I thought I wanted him to be, but I've grown to be more than just okay with that. He is the "steady" to my "bouncing off the walls excited." He is the "voice of reason" to my "crazy idea." He is the "calm, cool, collected" to my "emotional response." He's the "devil's advocate" to my "Let's just go for it!" He is the "peanut butter" to my "jelly"! He is the other half of the inside jokes that nobody else would understand. Because we were both willing to work on our relationship and embrace the changes we needed to make, our marriage was able to thrive.

But what do you do if you don't have friendships or a relationship like I just described? Maybe you moved across the country and left all your friends behind. Or maybe that person you thought was a dear friend showed their true colors and your friendship is now fractured. You're feeling the loneliness, the lack of support, or even simply not having someone in your corner rooting for you. How do you build new friendships or better relationships?

- Pray for your relationships. Pray for friends, and pray for healing.
- Commit to being a better friend or wife.
- Be proactive. Reach out. Connect through texting and social media. Make time to get together in person whenever possible.
- Cultivate the relationships you have now. Ask about each other's day, and take as much time, or more, to listen as you do when sharing.
- Develop a heart of thankfulness for the relationships that come your way.
- And remember, healthy relationships are good for the soul and are worth fighting for. Don't let an angry word or a disagreement ruin a friendship. Talk it out. Don't stuff your feelings.

Good friendships are worth searching for if you don't have them; they're worth fighting for if they're broken; and they're worth cultivating when you have them.

CHAPTER NINE
think outside the box

*"And these words that I command you today
shall be on your heart.
You shall teach them diligently to your children,
and shall talk of them when you sit in your house,
and when you walk by the way,
and when you lie down, and when you rise."
Deuteronomy 6:6–7 (ESV)*

BRAVE PARENTING

What do I do if my parents were not good examples?

What if I doubt my parenting skills?

What if I ruin my kids?

How can I be a better parent?

> Step outside the box. Give yourself grace. Trust your instincts. And be on your knees praying for your kids every day. Focus on the relationship.

Growing up, all I ever really wanted to be was a wife and mom. I remember in third grade playing at my friend's house pretending we were pregnant. Oh, the site we must have been walking down the street with beach towels stuffed under our t-shirts to create a large pregnancy bump. Thanks to my perfectionist personality, I mastered the art of shaping the towel into the perfect replica of a pregnant belly. We borrowed a couple of old purses from my friend's mom's closet, put on some hot pink lipstick, and waddled our "pregnant" selves out the door to circle the neighborhood for a few hours.

My imagination was pretty vivid during those years. I loved playing the board game Life just to see how many children I would end up with by the end of the game. I fantasized about growing up and marrying someone named Kevin, not a real crush by any means, but Kevin seemed like a good, strong name for my handsome future husband! I pictured three perfect children—a boy, a girl, and then another boy. I had three sisters, so it only seemed fitting that I would grow up to even out the ratio a bit by having more boys than girls.

Amid all this fantasy about my ideal future life, I was living out a less than ideal situation. As the child of divorce who spent more time with my dad and stepmom, I had all the usual insecurities and fears that many children in similar situations find themselves in. However, things were even tougher due to the lack of a deep relationship with my stepmom. She was fabulous at many things but relating and communicating with her children was not one of them. Her intentions were in the right place, but her execution was far out in left field. She baked memorable meals from scratch, taught us the beauty of gardening and growing fresh herbs, and was skilled at taking care of plants and finding the most gorgeous antiques, but she had no knack for connecting with us on a heart level.

In sixth grade, I wanted to ask my stepmom a few questions about sex, but her response brushed me aside. The following year, I had a crush on a boy and wished I could share a little bit about him with her, like I knew my friends did with their mothers. But I knew her response would be something like "You shouldn't be thinking about boys. You shouldn't have a crush. You don't need a boyfriend." I would not be met with understanding. There wouldn't be this giddy mother-daughter scene filled with laughing and giggling or a loving chat between a mom and daughter that might have played out between one of the teen characters and her mother on *90210*. There was no late-night conversation like the ones you see on *Gilmore Girls* between Lorelei and her daughter Rory. No, for me, a lecture would follow, and I would put up a wall. So, I learned that some things are better left unsaid. I am sure that, long before some of those seventh-grade memories, I learned that it was best to stuff my dreams, like I did my feelings. I continued dreaming about the family I would one day have, thinking about boys, and developing secret crushes, but I never shared anything real or deep with my stepmom. I did what I was told, learned how to keep the peace, but never truly connected or had a relationship with her.

Our house was an interesting paradox because, unlike my relationship with my stepmom, I had a fabulous father-daughter relationship with my dad. He saw me. He believed in me, and he knew I could dream big dreams. We had similar ways of thinking about things and often went for runs together and contemplated the meaning of life and what to expect in the afterlife.

The disconnect between my relationship with my stepmom

compared to my relationship with my dad centered around a concept regarding rules and relationship. When I was a teenager, I read a book with a great quote that I have clung to my whole life—"Rules without relationship leads to rebellion." At the time, I wasn't thinking about anything other than my frustrations with my circumstances, but as someone who frequently self reflects, reading that sentence was a major "ah-ha" moment.

What does "rules without relationship" mean? I wasn't one to get in trouble very much, actually it was pretty rare, but one instance the summer before my senior year comes to mind. One of my good friends was heading off to the military, and my boyfriend and I were invited to a going-away party at the friend's house. My boyfriend had had a couple of alcoholic drinks, and when we arrived, he was joking around with our friend's mom who smelled the alcohol on his breath. My parents were told about what had happened and that I rode in the car with him after he had been drinking, which was a huge no-no for obvious reasons.

Facing the consequences of the situation terrified me, but as our family worked through it and had conversations about it, the most eye-opening thing for me was my *internal* response. On the one hand, when thinking about how my stepmom was upset about the situation, my mind went down the road of "next time I will be more discrete" or "next time I will find a better way to not get caught." On the other hand, when thinking about my dad, no punishment or consequence seemed adequate. Just the realization that I had let him down was enough to have me *ground myself* for three months. Yes, you read that right. I grounded myself. I made the decision that I was not going to ask to go anywhere or do anything with friends. I felt sick to my stomach just knowing that I had disappointed my dad. I lost sleep knowing that I had not lived up to my values and commitments by riding in a car with someone who had been drinking alcohol.

That experience made it so clear to me that the mantra "Rules without relationship leads to rebellion" was so much more than a pretty sentence in a book. It accurately portrayed what I was living out. Plus, it made me realize that someday, when I became a parent, relationship would be paramount, and connection would be non-negotiable.

One Sunday, when I was about twenty years old and a few years before I had my kids, our pastor talked about a concept that stuck with me. He explained how anyone can be forced to behave a certain way, but it's what's on the inside that matters. After listening to his sermon, I realized all the ways that I had simply complied because it was the "right" thing to do and to avoid trouble.

A great example of rules versus relationship and simply doing something because it's the "right" thing is the black and white cartoon featuring the little boy named Johnny. One of the scenes shows a classroom and little Johnny refusing to sit down. His teacher repeatedly says, "Johnny, sit down. Johnny, sit down. Johnny, sit down." After a bit more prodding, Johnny finally sits down and raises his hand. When called upon, he addresses the teacher and says, "It may look like I'm sitting down, but just so you know, I'm standing up on the inside." Johnny did the right thing, but only because it was the rule, and not because he wanted to please and obey the teacher.

At twenty-two years old, right out of college, I landed my first job teaching high schoolers. Being able to live out another dream of mine thrilled me, and the concept of rules versus relationship was never far from my mind. Week after week, month after month, semester after semester, I found ways to weave the rules into the relationship. Of course, one must abide by school rules and classroom rules, but by taking an active approach to connect with every student, to show them how much I cared, and to really see them not just as a random student filling a seat but for who they were, the rules seemed much less important. I noticed that as I built the relationships the students followed the rules out of respect for me and our relationship rather than simply because of the threat of getting in trouble if they didn't.

During my second year of teaching, my first son was born in November. I had already had a couple of miscarriages, so my pregnancy was less than stress-free, to say the least. However, the second I met my baby boy, I knew I would move mountains and go to the ends of the earth to protect him, to love him, and to raise him to the best of my abilities. I also committed myself to focusing on relationship, no matter how many children God would bless me with. I had witnessed the benefits of building relationships firsthand while I was teaching, and I wanted that with my children. I didn't want to be the mom that only said "I told you so" or "because I said so." I wanted to be the mom whose kids understood the reason and knew the rules, guidelines, and boundaries were there because of love. Approaching parenting this way took a lot of bravery on my part and a lot of willingness to not just do what everybody else was doing.

It's sad for me to count how many times over the years that I thought about how I needed to do the complete opposite of what I had seen and experienced in a particular situation when I was growing up. Now that my oldest son has started his career, I can look back and see all the ways that my thinking outside the box helped. I remember when he was in fifth grade and plans were in place to show the puberty video at school. We had already had some talks about our bodies and how they were fearfully and wonderfully made, but I wanted to dive in a little deeper before he was taught any more from the school or any more from the kids on the bus, for that matter.

The problem was, when I was about eleven years old, the extent of the sex talk I received involved me asking the question "Do you have to take your shirt off when you have sex?" The simple answer was "You don't have to, but most people do," and I could tell by the tone of that reply that I shouldn't ask anymore. It wasn't until I was in seventh grade and spending time at a friend's house that the topic of sex came up. All I knew until that day was the answer to that *one* question I had asked, what I had guessed from random clips on TV, and that you wait until you're married. I was utterly mortified when my friend shared with me the details that her much older sister had taught her about what goes on during sex.

Fast forward quite a few years. I didn't want my son to experience the shame, guilt, and confusion about sex, pleasure, and God's design that I did, so I weaved a story in terms that he could understand. I told him how these Cadbury egg-shaped things called "ovaries" released eggs every month. The eggs were captured by the fallopian tubes, otherwise known as the "little water slides," and carried to the small uterus, aka the "neat little basket" waiting for the baby. We talked about periods, body hair, and all sorts of bodily functions that you know your prepubescent sons are about to experience. One of my goals was to make sure this conversation was as comfortable as possible. However, let's be real, I'm sure no young boy truly wants to have this conversation, but you wouldn't have known that by the way my oldest, and then my other three sons later on, reacted to the situation. Some of the other baseball moms heard about the conversation and asked me to have the sex talk with their sons too!

I committed to making sure my sons knew that God designed their bodies perfectly and that nothing they experienced was gross or unusual. I wanted them to have the utmost confidence in how their bodies were designed. I did not want them to think of sex as dirty even though I talked to them about waiting for marriage, saving themselves for their wives, and what the Bible says about purity. I wanted to make sure they knew their bodies were created to respond favorably, but in the right context. Now, all those topics weren't dumped into one conversation, and as the boys grew older, our conversations about sex and the human body went a little bit deeper than Cadbury eggs, water slides, and menstrual cycles.

My point is, by being open, addressing it directly, and creating a place where my sons felt that they could come to me with any questions about their body or about sex, we removed the taboo nature around this topic. My husband appreciated this approach although he was more than willing to let me be the one who had these often-surprising conversations.

The norm in most of society and relationships is for people to follow in their father or mother's footsteps for generation after generation. Why? Because most people model their choices after their own experiences, whether good or not. My experience with the sex talk as a child wasn't necessarily a good one, and I chose to break the generational pattern for my children. At my core, I had a longing for connection. I didn't want my children to turn eighteen, graduate, and move on without another thought. I wanted a relationship that could evolve from a basic parent-child relationship to a respectful adult friendship. But in order to have what I wanted, I had to break the generational pattern in some areas and make it about the relationship, not just the rules. Don't get me wrong, I have continued so many aspects of my upbringing with my own five children—the family movie nights, the special dinners, taking turns opening one present at a time on Christmas morning (We got this from my mom! She always wanted to savor each and every special moment of gift opening), and a whole list of other amazing memories that I carried from my childhood to my motherhood.

Brave parenting involves a lot of work. It involves truly loving each of your children the way they need to be loved. It involves setting boundaries but knowing how to create relationships through the process. It involves instilling a love for the Lord, confidence in themselves, a sense of incredible self-worth, a sense of purpose, and the belief that they can do anything they are called to do if they step out in faith and put feet to that faith. I did not sign up for eighteen years of simply creating rules for my kids in an effort to have them fall in line and to just "get through it." What I did sign up for was building that relationship and creating a deep, personal connection with each of my kids.

When my four boys were quite young, someone said to me, "Too bad you don't have a girl, because they are so different." I was perplexed at the time since each of my four boys was quite different from the others. My oldest son, Logan, is more of a talker. We go for walks and have long conversations. I am a safe place for him to over-analyze and go through every scenario when thinking through a decision that he needs to make. I am his sounding board as he sets goals for the future. We've grown to have a really special bond as he has become an adult, and we are often found walking on the beach discussing our callings on this earth and the ways God has shown favor and blessed our lives.

My second son, Mason, keeps to himself more than his older brother. His faith is strong, and his friend circle is tight. I have learned with him to be patient when I want to know what's on his mind or what his decision about any particular topic might be. I have found that pushing too hard makes things uncomfortable for him and puts us at odds with each other. By respecting his timeline and the way that he wants to communicate, our bond is stronger than ever. As his faith has deepened, so has our relationship.

My third son, Parker, is my most introverted child. He is easy-going, laid-back, and loves taking a deep dive into a good book or a full-on series. He's the child that could easily be overlooked if I allowed myself to get distracted with the busyness of the other four. With him, I take special care to make sure to ask him questions about what he's reading or what game he's playing so that we can connect and have a conversation. I want him to know that what interests him interests me. I want to make sure he knows that if it's important to him it's also important to me. He is such an example of loyalty and is a young man after God's own heart as he pursues his faith more deeply each year.

My fourth son, my little Owen, is my extroverted energizer bunny. He is the one that thrives off praises. He is the one that does so much better when I remind him often of what he's doing right and how he's succeeding rather than simply nagging about what he's left undone. He is quite strong-willed and can be stubborn, so it takes a little bit more care to navigate this early teenager. A hug and an "I appreciate you!" goes a long way with him. He's always good for a funny story!

And then there's my little girl. Hazel craves quality time, affection, and individual attention. It's easy with so much going on in a big family to get lost in all the conversations, but this sweet girl wants us to look her in the eye and participate in whatever story she's weaving. She wants to snuggle, and she wants some time just to play and have one of us all to herself. She has a tender little heart and a slightly shy spirit. She's not exceedingly emotional but does best when handled with gentleness and patience.

While I've stressed my commitment to connection and understanding—the building of the relationship—with each of my unique, designed by God, children, don't mistake that for letting my children walk all over me! I still make sure they know the rules that every one of us has in our family. One time I was in Target with Owen when he was five years old. We were in the checkout line and, of course, my cart was full of about fifty things that I hadn't put on my list. I mean, who can go to Target and just grab one or two things from a list? As we were standing there, Owen looked at me and asked if he could have a candy bar. I responded calmly, "Not today." Normally, my answer would have been enough for him, but not that day.

My sweet, angelic little five-year-old looked me in the eye and said, "If you don't buy me the candy that I want, I am going to scream my head off right now until you get it for me."

I looked around the store just like many moms would do in the same situation, except I wasn't looking around to help myself decide whether or not I was going to buy the candy. I was counting how many people might be annoyed by the intense screaming that was getting ready to erupt. I certainly was not going to be intimidated by my five-year-old child, and I was not going to reward his behavior with a candy bar either.

Honestly, I tried not to laugh when Owen said that he would scream his head off. I couldn't believe that a five-year-old could put into words the type of manipulation we've all witnessed. How many times have you seen a young child throwing a fit knowing that, if he screamed long enough, he would get what he wanted just so the screaming would stop? Now my child was explaining to me what that tantrum would look like and his plan for it to happen.

So, I looked him in the eye and calmly said, "Bring it. You're not getting the candy."

Well, for whatever reason, his tantrum never started. I had called his bluff, and he had seen that I meant business. His plan wasn't going to work with me. He knew the rule that when mom says no, she means no. He tried to push back and get his way, but it failed. This was a small victory but a victory, nonetheless. Other times the tantrums happened and the butting of heads began. However, consistency with the relationship was the key. Even at his tender age of five, I made sure to connect with Owen on a level that let him know that he truly mattered to me. His thoughts and wants were important. This didn't mean always saying "yes" as you just read, but it meant not having rules just for the sake of rules. He learned that mom had boundaries and limits and that they were there for good reasons. He learned that when mom said "no" it was for a purpose, not just to be the bad guy. Fast forward many years later, he occasionally has his moments of push-back as many teens do, but because we established loving, relationship-filled boundaries early on, he knows that rules are not there to punish but rather to guide.

Becoming the parent that you long to be is a process. I have changed so much over the fourteen years between my oldest and youngest child. By the time I had Hazel, my fifth child, my breastfeeding journey looked different, our family sleeping arrangements looked different, and Hazel's food habits were different than what I had done with her older brothers. Honestly, just about everything looked at least a little bit different than it had when I first became a mom. I don't have major regrets about things that I did with each of the boys, but I did evolve a little bit with each one. I have held on to the concept of "as we know better, we start to do better." As I grew older, learned more, spent time in Facebook groups, read more, and just gained more confidence in my mother's intuition, my convictions about raising my daughter grew. It's been really fun to parent her as a preschooler while having teenage sons at the same time. I have been able to relive so many things through her and be reminded of things we did when the boys were her age. I'm making fun memories with my little girl at the same time that I am watching my relationship with my sons mature as they pass into adulthood. How cool is that?

Earlier I mentioned that looking at my past a little bit and identifying some of the gaps and things that were missing helped me carve my path as a mother. As I studied my past, I discovered ways I was hurt or felt lost, and I also recalled some parenting moments from my childhood that could have been handled better, like the sex talk or the lack of one. Take some time to stop and think about your childhood. You likely already have some things in your life that you don't want to repeat with your children. You also probably have things that you experienced or witnessed in other families that are *healthy* parenting habits that you want to emulate. Write down the things you *don't* want to repeat and the healthy habits you want to add. Parenting starts by being open-minded and willing to grow with each passing month.

As moms, we are going to have some of those moments that I call "not so proud mommy moments." I've had times when I've lost my cool or didn't handle a situation the way I would've liked. I have to remind myself that it's not okay to beat myself up over things that seemed like a good idea at the time but weren't. I don't need to feel guilty over the past, but I do need to embrace the ways I have grown as a mother. You may not always have it all together, but you can forgive yourself when you have those less than perfect moments. In those moments, I am reminded of God's grace, and that motherhood is not about being perfect. You see, you may not feel like you are the perfect mom, but you are the perfect mom for *your* kids. You were chosen for them, and they were chosen for you. Give yourself permission to make mistakes as a mom. I have found that my kids remember the LEGO towers, the four-wheeler rides, the days playing in the water, and not so much the random times when mom was more frustrated than usual or took the easy way out.

Sometimes you need to change course and say "this is not working for me"—and that's okay. I remember being encouraged to try the "cry it out" method of sleep training with my oldest son. I know many people embrace this and other similar methods for getting their children to sleep, but I realized early on that this method just didn't make sense for our family. I didn't know anyone who co-slept with their children, but I felt that it might be a better method for us. I stepped out in faith that I would be able to do what was best for our family.

Sometimes you need to apologize to your children. I remember when Logan, my oldest, was four years old, and my husband and I were taking a class at church that talked a lot about "speaking scripture" to your children. I had quoted to Logan different passages from Proverbs about fools, folly, anger, and other behaviors. One day I raised my voice at him, and I felt so guilty for losing my cool. I went back to his room a little bit later to apologize.

"Logan," I said, "There is no excuse for my frustration and for the yelling that just happened. I want to tell you that I'm sorry and ask you to forgive me."

"I forgive you, Mom. Don't worry, I know you were just being a fool."

Out of the mouths of babes. He used scripture right back at me!

There is bravery when you step out in faith and carve your own parenting story. *You* know what your kids need most. *You* know what makes sense for their unique personalities. And *you* know what fits with the mold of your family. Don't be afraid to walk a different path than your sister, brother, mother, your best friend, or moms in your social media circle. Step outside the box. You need to do you. Give yourself grace. Trust your instincts. And be on your knees praying for your kids every single day. Focus on the *relationship*.

CHAPTER TEN

tell your story

"For I know the plans I have for you," declares the Lord,
"plans to prosper you and not to harm you,
plans to give you hope and a future.
Then you will call on my and come and pray to me,
and I will listen to you."
Jeremiah 29:11–12 (NIV)

BRAVE FAITH

What do I do if I feel like I can't go on
when my dreams are destroyed?

Does my story really matter to someone else?

> Take the next step. Just do the next right thing for your situation. One foot in front of the other. Day by day. Inch by inch.

TELL YOUR STORY

MOST LITTLE GIRLS HAVE DAYDREAMS and wild imaginations about what their life will look like when they grow up. With three younger sisters and a handful of school friends, I can tell you that we filled our days with conversations about all sorts of big plans that we envisioned. We talked about weddings. We spoke about our future children and fantasized about houses and Rocky Mountain vacations. What we didn't talk about were divorces, adultery, abusive relationships, lack of income, job changes, infertility, cross-country moves, losing loved ones too soon, and all the social injustices and sadness that fill our news screens and social media pages every single day. As kids, we were innocent and full of hope. The future looked vast, beautiful, and full of incredible possibilities. Then, real life happened.

For me personally, one of the biggest reality checks as an adult was our fertility journey. People often make jokes about how my husband might "look at me and I get pregnant" because they see that we have five amazing children. When we announced our pregnancy with our fourth son, we had lots of "you know how this happens, right?" I would smile and laugh a little while thinking to myself "You have NO idea what we have been through, and if you did, you wouldn't think this is funny." We all know that what you see isn't always the whole picture, right?

My first pregnancy started with incredible waves of nausea and vomiting, which they say can be a sign of a healthy pregnancy. The moment I found out I was pregnant I knew what the saying "a mother's love" actually meant. I didn't have to wait to see my baby's face to be fiercely protective and already head-over-heels in love. I was smitten. And then at the end of my first trimester, the hemorrhaging started, and the bargaining with God began. I sat outside on the concrete steps behind my house, underneath the starry Nebraska sky, sobbing and praying out loud to God. "Lord, please spare my child. Don't let me lose this baby. I will do anything. I will raise him right. I will love him unconditionally, even if he is not born perfect, but please don't take my baby." I felt very alone, just me and my baby. I was in my early twenties and didn't have any friends with kids or know anyone who had gone through anything like this before. A few weeks later, it was all over, and I was convinced that my body had failed me.

I grew up through that experience. I grieved for my baby, whom I named Samuel. Even though I never got to see his face, he was a person to me. He was a life. He had a soul.

My second pregnancy started a bit differently. The nausea wasn't as bad, and there was no bleeding. I was hopeful that I would have a different outcome this time. I convinced myself that my first miscarriage had been a heartbreaking "fluke of nature" as the doctor referred to it. He told me it was like a puzzle that was just missing a few pieces. And then, at a late first-trimester ultrasound, our second baby no longer had a heartbeat. I was devastated.

At that point, the doctor decided to do some testing since, at my young age, two miscarriages so close together might have a cause. They determined that our second baby was a healthy baby girl. We named her Hope because the testing they performed after my losing her gave me hope that we would find answers. Answers that would allow us to find our way to having a healthy baby. During my third pregnancy, the doctor prescribed hormone supplements to see if those might help. I added in a healthy dose of prayer because I had seen my God perform miracles, and prayer felt like all I had at the time.

So many times, pregnancy forums and blog posts talk about

how safe a pregnancy is once it reaches the stage where you see your baby's heartbeat. However, that stage was never very reassuring for me. Of course, I loved the sound of the rapid thumping heartbeat, but, because both of my losses had been after a heartbeat, I knew the heartbeat was no guarantee.

All through my third pregnancy, I had a paradox of emotions. On the one hand, I was thrilled with each milestone, thrilled with each reassuring ultrasound, and, of course, thrilled every single time I felt my baby move, kick, flip, and do whatever those babies do in there! But I also had this persistent feeling of "When was the other shoe going to drop?" That feeling made it very hard to be 100 percent excited. I found myself so very jealous of other pregnant women. I watched them announce their pregnancies early and then joyfully breeze through the whole nine months. My sister Jillian was pregnant with her first at around the same time, and I was envious that she was not worried about losing her baby and was simply able to experience the joy and the pregnancy glow without the incessant worry.

I found myself in a constant internal battle. I would ask myself, "Is worrying going to change things?" Maybe, but only if I believed that if I worried it would be less painful if something happened, which I knew wasn't true. It wasn't like I thought to myself during one of my miscarriages, "Whew…I am SOOO glad that I've been worrying because this is waaaay easier now. I am glad that I've been thinking about this!" No. It was gut-wrenching. And a part of me just couldn't completely let go of the worry.

At the end of my pregnancy with my oldest son Logan, I started feeling "off" and was almost made fun of by my doctor. He chalked up everything I said to being a newly expectant mother. He finally caved, gave me an ultrasound, and called me later telling me to urgently get to the hospital. It turned out my mother's intuition was right—there was no measurable fluid around the baby. It was time to labor and get him out. Twenty-seven hours later and with an emergency C-section under my belt, my eight-pound-seven-ounce beautiful baby boy was born. The moment they pulled him through my incision and held up a mirror to show me his little face, I exclaimed loudly for all the surgical team to hear "Oh my gosh! It's a real baby, and we get to *keep* it!" It was as if reality hit me at that moment. This was true. This was real. This was a miracle. My miracle. My baby. In my arms.

Two years later, I went into labor with my second son, Mason, five weeks before my due date. Nowadays, five weeks early is not concerning for lots of babies. We see twenty-five-week preemies, and some even earlier, who do very well after extended NICU stays. So, imagine our surprise when our five-week premature little man ended up fighting for his life in the NICU. I will never forget the neonatologist telling my husband that our son had a ten percent chance of survival because his lungs were not ready. I will never forget the NICU nurse, who had worked at the hospital for thirty years, crying over my baby's incubator. Once Mason turned the corner, he improved quickly, but his stay in the NICU was one of the most difficult things Brent and I had ever gone through. Watching the ventilators, all the tubes, IVs, pic lines, and procedures made me realize how good I had it the first time since my son Logan was strong and healthy and right next to me when I left the hospital. When Mason was three months old, we ended back up in the hospital as he battled RSV and pneumonia, and we once again hit our knees praying for his health.

My next pregnancy seemed to be going off without a hitch until

I hit thirty-seven weeks and needed to have an ambulance come get me due to what the doctors thought was a stroke. Thankfully, all ended up being just fine with the birth of our third son, but it was certainly a scary experience.

During my pregnancy with our fourth son, Owen, we found out early that we had been pregnant with twins and lost one. This loss was sad but felt different since we hadn't even known about the second baby nor had we seen the heartbeat. I named Owen's lost twin Eli and certainly think of him when I think about our babies in heaven. Things went smoothly with the rest of the pregnancy after we finished the first trimester, well, other than Owen being ten-pounds-thirteen-ounces and making this mama miserable for eight-and-a-half months.

After Owen's birth is when I made my decision to have my tubes tied. In Chapter Five, Let Go—Brave Surrender, I talk extensively about the loss of our baby girl Faith several years after Owen was born. If you haven't read that chapter yet, you'll definitely get a glimpse into another piece of our fertility journey.

About six months after we lost Faith, I took another pregnancy test. I tested about five days earlier than I should have, but I couldn't hold off any longer. At 5 a.m., with my glasses out of reach, I squinted at the faintest pink line on the test. Was I really seeing what I thought I was? It was positive! In that moment, I was overwhelmed with fear, excitement, hope, and love. I woke Brent up to tell him the news and then spent the rest of the day in a haze of emotions with a huge grin on my face.

When I was six weeks pregnant, we saw not one but two little heartbeats on the ultrasound screen. After such a long journey over fourteen years that included so many ups and downs, to say we were elated about welcoming twins hardly describes the feeling. I couldn't believe, after everything we had been through, that I was going to become a mom of six kids! I was so excited that these two babies would have each other considering their four brothers were quite a bit older—our youngest was seven at the time. I started dreaming of all the fun things that the twins would do together and how much fun it would be for them to have a sibling the same age.

As a breastfeeding mom, I was excited to take on the challenge of breastfeeding multiples and began ordering books, following blogs, and immersing myself in the world of mothering multiples. Since I had given away all my maternity clothes years before, I bought so many cute shirts with sayings such as "Got twins?" and "Keep calm it's just twins." I hung the cute maternity shirts in my closet, dove into my stack of books, and joyfully embarked on the journey of twin motherhood.

We breathed a small sigh of relief after we exited a complicated first trimester. I found myself relaxing a bit and finding my groove in juggling the boys while being pregnant and taking care of my needs and my unborn babies who I assumed were likely twin boys. At one of our second-trimester ultrasounds—and you have a lot of ultrasounds when you are carrying multiples—the screen revealed, much to our surprise, or shock, to be more accurate, that both babies were girls. We were having twin girls! I hadn't been on a quest to get the girl like some people often asked us, but after four boys, you assume that boys are all you make! These two little girls would not only have the incredible experience of simply being twins sisters, but my four sons would have the awesome responsibility of being big brothers to these two little girls.

One day, I stood at our sliding glass door looking out at our acreage, our swimming pool, and the fun play structure that hadn't been used quite as much the last few years. I had images of two little girls running around in sundresses, ponytails, and squealing in delight as they played tag and raced up the steps to the tornado slide. I was *all in* and experiencing a motherhood glow. I was pregnant with two little miracles and I was not taking that for granted.

At another second-trimester ultrasound, our world shattered. Although "Baby A" was healthy and active, "Baby B" no longer had a heartbeat. I started hyperventilating and sobbing, and my husband stood up and said some things that I don't need to repeat in this book as he expressed his heartbreak and grief.

The whole way home from that appointment I sobbed. I could not even bring myself to have the conversation with my siblings, so I sent a simple text telling them what had happened. That was all I could muster. I was overwhelmed with emotion and grief. I dreaded telling our sons, ages seven, nine, eleven, and thirteen, that one of their baby sisters had died. They had accompanied me to several ultrasounds before and watched the babies jumping around having a party inside of mom. I knew the news would crush them, and it was more than I wanted their little hearts to experience.

The moment we arrived home, I packed up all the maternity shirts that referenced twins. I put all the books about multiples in a drawer in my bedroom. I couldn't even bring myself to look out the sliding glass door toward our backyard playground because all

I could think about was that there would never be two. So many reminders were everywhere.

As you can imagine, I found myself unable to sleep that night. At three o'clock in the morning, I quietly walked through the house trying to miss the noisiest boards in our wood floors so that I didn't wake everyone. I worked my way downstairs to my son Mason's room, who was eleven at the time. He was my most sensitive, intuitive child, and he had a way of showing me so much love. I climbed into his twin bed with him, and when I felt him stir, I simply said, "I am just so sad."

I felt his little hand reach out to hold mine, and he said, "I am too, Mom."

I cried myself to sleep next to him that night.

Grieving this loss was like nothing I had ever experienced before. The conflicting emotions tore my heart in two. There were moments when I experienced such intense grief followed by guilt. I felt guilty for being so sad about the loss when I felt like I should be focusing on the fact that I still had another beautiful baby growing inside of me. People would say "Well, at least you have one still" which bothered me because if a parent loses a child in a car crash, we don't say "Well, at least you have a few more at home." I felt guilty for grieving the loss of Baby B while my daughter Hazel ("Baby A") was growing perfectly. Other days I felt so excited to meet Hazel and felt very happy at that moment in my pregnancy only to have a cloud of guilt come over me for experiencing joy when I felt like I should be experiencing sadness over the loss of "Baby B," whom we named Bea.

When my water broke prematurely, I delivered both babies via C-section seven weeks early. That joyous moment of hearing Hazel's cries had twinges of sadness as I held my tiny baby Bea wrapped in a blanket. I told her how much we loved her and how sad we were not to experience life with her on this earth. And then, before a nurse took Bea away, I promised her I would meet her again one day.

※

While we are on earth, we live in a broken world filled with pain and heartache. We can choose to see the bright side of things. We can choose to sit with our pain and to heal. We can choose to have faith to keep going each day even when things don't make sense. When I look at each of my pregnancy and loss stories all written out, I can't help but think to myself, "Wow, that was A LOT, but we kept going. We kept persevering. We continued to trust."

Honestly, the only thing that got me through all these times was my faith in the Lord. I have faith that He guides me, whether or not I understand how and why life takes some of its twists and turns. If I had seen the whole path ahead of me, would I have had the courage to continue, knowing the outcome? I am not sure, but I am grateful that God didn't ask me to look at the whole path and then decide. He just asked me to trust Him and take the next step.

The biggest piece of advice that I can give you as you travel through some murky waters is to just take the next step. Just do the next right thing for your situation. One foot in front of the other. Day by day. Inch by inch. Maybe your burden to bear is having lost someone close to you unexpectedly. Maybe it's the unknown of infertility. Maybe your biggest challenge is a history of broken relationships and broken trust. Stay the course. It's okay to not always have all the answers. It's perfectly fine to have to take a leap of faith sometimes. Or even *lots* of times. It's okay to cry. It's okay to feel.

One thing that helped me, that I hope helps you, was stopping the comparison game. Comparing my circumstances to those around me never got me anywhere. I shared the details of each of my stories with you because I wanted to give you a glimpse behind the curtain. On social media, people see my beautiful beach pictures with our five kids. They see the silly antics that I share and the fun times that we have. And all of that is true. All of that is real, but as you know from your own life experiences, social media can often be the highlight reel. For me, it was easy to look right and look left and then wonder, "Why me? Why did I lose another baby and she's never lost one? Why does she get to be happy and carefree during her pregnancy, but I can't be?" But all that served to do was break my heart more and instill fear. Rather than looking right and looking left, I had to choose to look up to the only One who could change my future. Then, I fixed my gaze toward the future laid out for me and took a big step.

We all have a choice when faced with things in life that leave us hopeless. When we feel stuck in our circumstances. When we don't see an obvious answer. When we feel like maybe this is our "lot in life." When we wonder if things will ever get better. We all have a choice. We can either throw up our hands and say. "Well, I guess this is just how it's going to be!" or we can trust that there is something bigger out there for us. We can chase our brave in those moments and say, "In spite of what's going on around me, I choose bravery. Even though this isn't the way I would have chosen, I will have courage in the face of adversity. I may not like the way this feels, and I might even feel a little gypped, but I don't get to choose everything that happens to me. However, I can choose how I react to my circumstances. I can choose to go through hard things, or I can choose to grow through hard things." At the end of the day, life is about lots of choices. Life is about how we react and whether or not we make lemonade out of the lemons tossed our way.

We all have a unique story that matters. I look back, because they say hindsight is 20/20, and I see how these hard times, these sometimes hopeless moments, these thousands of tear-filled nights, can now be used for good. Because the Lord asked me to walk through this valley of loss, premature babies, and all the uncertainty, I am now able to use this story for good. I am able to tell you that you are not alone. I am able to share with women that there is hope on the other side of fear, uncertainty, and hopelessness. I am able to wrap my arms around a friend, and say "I love you, and I feel your pain."

Each of us is living out a one-of-a-kind story that is uniquely ours. Think about people in your life that inspire you. Think about people whom you look up to. Why do you look up to them? What is so inspiring about their story? Are you inspired because they overcame something daunting? Are you inspired by something that they have achieved? Whatever it might be, I can tell you this—you are inspired and motivated because they have gone through something and came out on the other side triumphant. They have survived, thrived, and are proof that we can do hard things.

Going through the trials that you are facing will inspire someone that you likely don't even know is watching you. You will have empathy, words of wisdom, and make a lasting impact on others because of how you get through the dark times in your life. Perseverance, when there is no perfect plan laid out, will strengthen you.

You have everything it takes, but it's going to take everything you've got. The biggest blessings and "wins" in my whole life, whether in business, family, relationships, education, you name it, have come from persevering through the tough stuff, from digging deep and having courage. Our God is a big God who will do amazing things for us when we humble ourselves and trust his will above ours.

Your story matters. Be brave and tell it.

CHAPTER ELEVEN
choose all of it

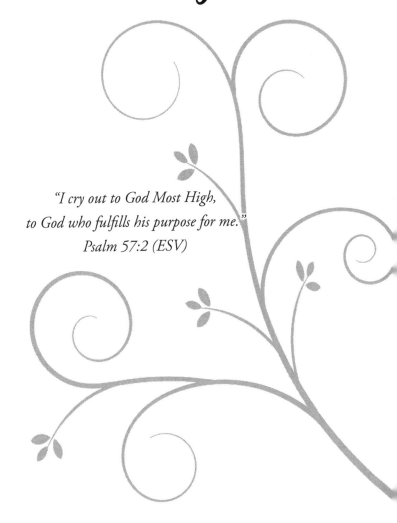

*"I cry out to God Most High,
to God who fulfills his purpose for me."
Psalm 57:2 (ESV)*

BRAVE PURPOSE

Is it okay if I pursue dreams besides being a mother?

Is it okay to want more?

Is it okay to pursue hobbies and dreams
outside of what others expect of me?

> Your story—the impact you were born to have—
> is created one brave step at a time,
> one brave moment, one threshold crossed.

As the oldest girl in my family, I naturally inherited some mothering instincts. I'll never forget being in the delivery room with my stepmom for my youngest sister's birth. I was beaming from ear to ear as I ran out into the waiting room to tell my siblings that our little sister, Kate, was here. We lived in a big old house, and my new little sister shared the front room on the second floor with me. Her iron crib was right next to my bed although she often ended up cuddled up with me in my queen-sized bed full of cozy, oversized quilts. When Kate was five, and after everyone else had taken their turn trying unsuccessfully to teach her to ride a bike, I finally had my turn. Within minutes, she was joyfully peddling around the neighborhood, and I found myself upstairs in my room crying my eyes out. I felt like she was mine and my baby was growing up way too fast. (This was a foreshadowing of the feelings I would have over and over as my own five kids would grow up too fast someday!) My stepmom and my little sister found me crying a little while later. Between the sobs I managed to choke out the words, "She's…just…so…BIG…she was JUST a baby…and now she's riding a bike!"

My stepmom consoled me and then looked into Kate's bright blue eyes and said, "Did you know Aspen was with you from the very beginning? She was in the delivery room when you were born."

Without missing a beat, my little sister patted our mom's leg, and in her most reassuring voice said, "I know. And don't worry, Mom, you were there, too!"

My little sister and I had an incredible bond, as I did with my other siblings, that bred a desire in me to nurture, support, and love on others. I worked hard to be there for them every step of the way and be a mentor as much as I could. Those early years of being the oldest sister, truly connecting and falling in love with being there for my siblings, watching them grow and step out of their comfort zones, and comforting them when they fell filled a huge need in me. It also created a desire to pursue anything in life that allowed me to be around others, impact others, and make a difference. By the time I was fifteen, I knew that my love of kids and teaching others was going to shape a huge part of my future. During my freshman year, I decided to pursue a career in teaching, and once I had children of my own, I planned to take a leave of absence.

My career path took several twists and turns along the way, but being there for others was always at the center. After college, I taught high school students, and then, as a stay-at-home mom, I ran a home daycare, followed by a cleaning business, and finally, I took the plunge into the world of network marketing, now often referred to as "social marketing." Yep, I joined one of *those* home-based business things.

I never pictured myself building a home-based business selling skin care products and makeup because, let's face it, I was relatively shy, lived in the middle of a cornfield, and had three boys ages three and under at the time. However, one Sunday, a friend from church shared an opportunity with me, and through all my skepticism, I said "yes" about joining the business. What hooked me was the option to choose my own schedule and let my work ethic determine my paycheck each month. Social media didn't exist to help me share my new business and its products, but somehow I believed that I could and would be successful. I was willing to copy what other people were doing in my company because I figured success leaves clues, and I would follow those ladies who were where I wanted to be. Before long, I envisioned relieving some of the financial pressure off my husband and taking vacations with my kids. I dreamed really big dreams of being that mom who would be able to say "yes" a lot more to my kiddos.

Over the course of ten years, I ended up climbing to some of the highest ranks in three different companies, leading thousands of people in network marketing, and building massive organizations of incredible people. Before starting my own company, I was hired for a corporate position in one of the largest network marketing companies in the world. Each of those steps along the way was big, bold, and scary. Going from a shy mom running a daycare to standing in front of a large group of women talking about products and my company was a huge leap.

Leading a much larger organization in my second company and teaching in front of thousands of people at conventions around the country caused me so much fear, but it led to so much growth. I will never forget the first time I was asked or rather *told* that I would be speaking on stage at an event and sharing my story of success in business while juggling motherhood. The plan was for me to teach everyone how they could follow in my footsteps. The big day arrived, and I felt like I had a huge pit in my stomach. I was terrified to go out on stage, and I was on the verge of hyperventilating. I was the only speaker who elected *not* to have the microphone that attached near the ear with the small microphone positioned right in front of the mouth. I asked for a handheld microphone because my breathing was so heavy and I was positive no one would be able to hear my words over my anxious breathing! My mentor, trying to encourage me as I walked to the stage, whispered, "You'll do great! Just do not go over the thirty minutes and you better crush it!" No pressure! But I did it.

Here's the thing, even with all the unknowns, I grew so much as a leader during that time. Stepping into a corporate position and then later as an *owner of my own network marketing company* were huge leaps. They each had the potential for great rewards, but it took everything I had to say "yes" and take the plunge of faith toward the next step.

When I looked back, as oftentimes lessons are learned and understood as we look backward and see the past, I realized something very profound:

If you had told that shy fifteen-year-old girl who decided to become a Spanish teacher one day that she would own a global company that would be a shining light and filled with a community of like-minded people daring enough to stand out in passion and purpose, she would have been terrified.

If you had told her that someday she would stream videos on Facebook and speak live in front of thousands, she would have told you that you were crazy and that she was unqualified.

If she had seen the big picture, she would have likely been too scared to take that first step of faith. She would have hesitated at the first open door.

However, God didn't show fifteen-year-old me the whole big plan for my life. He didn't show me all the different steps in my career that would be stops along the road to my final destination. He didn't tell me about all the huge personal growth opportunities that I would have to work through in order to be the person that He needed me to be for all those who would join my teams and then my company Bravenly Global. He just opened the very next door. He called me to take ONE step at a time into the unknown and trust that He would give me the strength. He reminded me that when I stayed in His will that He would not only equip me, but He would reveal more and more of His purpose and plan for my life.

How divinely orchestrated is it that the girl who battled feelings of unworthiness has been called to lead women all around the world and teach them every day how to believe in themselves? That little girl inside of me has spent her whole life battling those feelings of unworthiness, and she's spent so much time trying to perform, excel, succeed, and matter in this world. It has taken years for me to realize and live in the truth that I matter just because I exist. I am worthy because the Lord says I am. God called this shy girl to follow Him bravely into a career, or more accurately, a calling where she pours into women and shows them their worth and value every single day. My life's work revolves around making sure women around me know that they matter, they are capable, they are strong, and they are brave. I seek to empower them to take brave leaps of faith and live a courageous hope-filled life.

God has a purpose for your life as well. You might not clearly see that purpose every day while you're in the middle of life's messiness. And you may be like me and struggle with some of the guilt surrounding motherhood and juggling so many of the other roles in your life. I used to feel so torn heading out of the house at night for a meeting with my team members or my mentors. I was torn between wanting to spend time with my kids and knowing that I needed to get to an event to grow my business to the highest of highs and to grow myself as a leader. I spent a lot of time feeling guilty about *enjoying* the meetings, my team, sales, and my friends in the business. I felt like maybe there was something wrong with me that

I had this pull to have more, do more, and be more than only a wife and a mom.

Here is what God showed me: In order to be the best wife, mom, and the example I longed to be, I needed to do brave things. I needed to trust in His purpose and know that building my business and becoming a mentor, coach, CEO, and founder were not in *conflict* with the call He placed on my life to be a mother and wife, but rather they were *parallel* to that calling. It was not one or the other. I was not being asked to choose, which is what I *felt* that I needed to do. The answer was that I was simultaneously being asked to raise my children in the way that they should go and be my husband's life partner and companion all while working from home and pouring my heart into those around me.

By following my calling, I showed my kids each day what it meant to be brave, what courage looks like, and what following your passions is all about. I demonstrated what it looks like to pick yourself back up after you've been knocked down—which has happened more times than I wish it had! My kids watched a mom not take "no" for an answer. They learned from a mom who was on a mission. They saw the women around me making bold changes and pursuing bold dreams and how those decisions impacted their families' finances and futures as well.

I will never forget the day I had a conversation with my son Mason, who was fifteen and a freshman in high school at the time. I didn't expect him to know what he wanted to study in college or pursue as a profession, but we were discussing the topic anyway. He was talking through various scenarios and sharing some things that had interested him over the past couple of years when he said the words that struck such a powerful chord within me and inspired a major revelation. He said, "I am not quite sure what I want to do yet, but I want to do something that I am truly *passionate* about." Read that again. A fifteen-year-old boy literally said that he wanted to pursue something in life that he was passionate about. In my years of teaching high school Spanish, I never encountered a boy who so clearly knew the importance of following your passions.

In that moment, and in dozens more that would follow, I received my first glimpse of what chasing my brave for all those years had done for my children. Later conversations with several of my children continued to reveal the ways that they had been impacted by what they observed in my life and my husband's life as we both chose entrepreneurial paths. They watched as we picked ourselves back up and trusted the doors that the Lord sometimes slammed for us and the windows that He opened. They didn't blame me for the random nights away at meetings that I had beat myself up over when they were little. Instead, they were inspired and completely confident in their ability to pursue the life of their dreams, God-sized dreams, and not settle for less.

No one gets to tell you what you get to dream about, what you need to do to fulfill your calling, and what that missing piece is for you. It's okay to want more, need more, and pursue more. That tug toward more may very well be from God, especially if you've prayerfully considered His will. You may feel like you are being pulled in a scary direction because it's something you've never known before and it might take a skill you don't have yet or money that you need to raise. Whatever that thing is for you, I would encourage you to first lean into it, stay on your knees about it, be open to what might be next for you, and then when that last bit of clarity happens—jump.

Bravely chase your brave in the direction of your purpose. When you sometimes fall, and you will fall, just keep moving forward. I've never regretted the times that I took a step forward, or even twenty steps forward, and landed on my rear. I mean that. Sure, I've weathered the storms of businesses crashing and the let-downs in certain relationships, but the lessons I learned were completely priceless and inarguably necessary for me to be who God has called me to be. Keep on going. Keep saying yes to yourself and your dreams, and start saying no to the things in your life that don't align with your purpose and plan. You often have to say no to the "okay," "ho-hum," and even "good" things around you to have room on your plate and in your schedule to pursue the "great" things and the things dreams are made of.

Dare to dream the biggest dreams. Keep centered and staring straight ahead following the light that is leading you. There's no need or any benefit at all from comparing yourself to anyone around you. They aren't you. They aren't supposed to be in your line of sight right now. Your purpose is not the same as mine, but your purpose is 100 percent where you should be steering your ship. Your end game is what is supposed to be.

Your story—the impact you were born to have—is created one brave step at a time, one brave moment, one threshold crossed. Those steps take courage, and in retrospect, you will see that courage you mustered up and how God divinely guided your steps to create your story that matters. It's your turn, my friend.

find your purpose

be brave

choose all of it

acknowledgments

WRITING A BOOK IS MORE difficult and more rewarding than I ever could have imagined. None of this would have been possible without my husband, Brent, making sure that I could slip away and write, write, write. He's been my rock for over twenty years, and he has encouraged me to go after my big, bold, and often scary dreams. I did then, and I still do.

I am so grateful for my five kids and the way each of them has inspired me to be the best version of myself and to "show up" as my best self each and every day. I am so proud of the incredible people they are growing up to be! Keep your eyes on Jesus, kids! That is my wish for you!

A special thanks to Kara Starcher for being more than just an amazing editor but also a fabulous friend. You made sense of so many of my thoughts and feelings and helped bring *Chase Your Brave* to life! You helped craft this all so eloquently.

Thank you to my mom and Ben for suggesting that I write a book someday and believing that I had a story worth telling. You've been there through the ups and downs of my life and have demonstrated commitment, incredible work ethic, and unconditional love that have inspired me to be a better wife, mom, business owner, and friend.

Thank you to my dad for a lifetime of cheering me on and pouring belief into me any chance you could. I have always known you were in my corner and saw my potential even when I didn't. Thank you for being the person I could turn to in my darkest days and that always pointed me back to Jesus. Thank you for supporting my dreams all the years.

To my mother-in-law, Connie, there are no words to describe what your support has meant to me for all these years. You raised an incredible son, and you love our kids so well. You've always lovingly supported the paths we have taken, offered encouraging words, and been a wonderful sounding board in so many ways.

So many of these *Chase Your Brave* moments wouldn't have happened without the support of so many fabulous friends who have picked me up, set me straight, and kicked me in the behind when I have needed it. Ashley Walmer, you have carried me through some valleys and experienced some of my most thrilling moments. Your support and willingness to "sell paper plates" with me makes me smile and humbles my heart in ways I cannot describe. Dani Bretz, you've been a vault for my deepest thoughts. You've been a sounding board for some of my wildest ideas, and you've always been steady and true. Without you, I'd be less of me.

To my sisters Jillian, Ashley, and Kate, where would any of us be without each other? We chased our brave as little girls, and I am so very proud of each of you! I am inspired by *your* bravery and perseverance as you've weathered life's challenges of motherhood, single motherhood, cross-country moves, job changes, college, and all the other things life has thrown your way. You have grown through it all and shown the world what it means to stare fear in the face and then

ACKNOWLEDGMENTS

push right past it because you refuse to let it hold you back. The root and foundation of who I am starts right there with the three of you. Love you to pieces!

A huge thanks and a big hug to everyone who is a part of Bravenly Global, now and in the future! You are my inspiration, and building a company for you, and with you, is one of my "biggest braves"! I will keep chasing my brave and standing upon the pillars of Courage, Integrity, and Impact to continue creating a place for each of you to *shine* and realize your biggest dreams. You are creating a ripple effect of change that will leave a legacy far beyond business and great products. You are a difference maker, and you matter to me. I am forever grateful!

To other friends, colleagues, and family, including Shelly Williamson, Stephanie and Jennifer Emry, Cody Houston, Malerie McNair, Molly Paez, and so many more, thank you for being a part of this journey of my life. You've shaped me in ways that I cannot even describe. You mean the world to me and have pushed me to be brave.

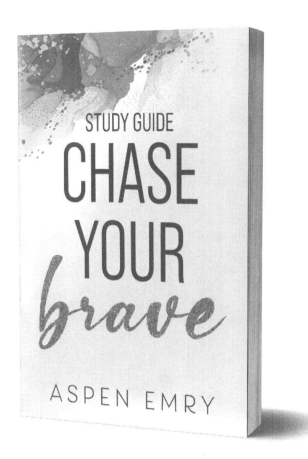

DIGITAL DOWNLOAD AVAILABLE AT
CHASEYOURBRAVE.COM

Take the message of *Chase Your Brave* deeper and discover how to apply it to your everyday life.

PERFECT FOR INDIVIDUAL OR GROUP STUDY

about the author

ASPEN EMRY WAS RAISED OUTSIDE of Lincoln, Nebraska, and now resides in Florida. She considers her faith, family, and friends to be the three most important things in her life. As a former schoolteacher turned entrepreneur, speaker, and author, Aspen considers it her life mission to serve others, to empower women to take brave steps in their lives, and to help them see their inherent worthiness. If she's not working actively with her Brand Partners at her company Bravenly Global, she can be found with her husband, Brent, and five children, Logan, Mason, Parker, Owen, and Hazel, walking on the beach, traveling, or simply enjoying time together.